50 Ways
To Use Your
Noodle

Loads Of Land Games
With Foam Noodle Toys

Chris Cavert
Sam Sikes

Copyright© 1997 by Chris Cavert & Sam Sikes
ISBN   0-9646541-1-3

Learning Unlimited Corporation
5155 East 51st, Suite 108
Tulsa, OK 74135
(918) 622-3292   fax (918) 622-4203

Printed in the United States of America

Table of Contents

PROBLEM-SOLVING ACTIVITIES

Acknowledgements

We gathered the materials and ideas for *50 Ways To Use Your Noodle* very quickly. It was amazing how willing game players that we admire shared their ideas so freely. It says a lot about their character and zest for life.

We'd like to thank the following people (in no particular order) for their game contributions: Craig Dobkin, Karl Rohnke, Mike Spiller, Jim Cain, Renny Cavener, Clay Fiske, Teresa Ostrander, and the staff at Camp Lutherhoma.

A sincere thank you goes to all the people who braved the exposure and let us include them in the photos. They are Mary, Mary Ann, Sara, Renny, "Hobbs", Patty, Paul, Eileen, Wayland, Mary Beth, Jeff, Chris, Ned, Jacob, Zack, TWU S.O.L.s, Nathan, Leslee, Stan, Devin, Laura, Angie, Alisha, Shanda, CeCe, Stan, TOTO Kansas '97 gamesters. We appreciate Sharon for gathering kids for the shoot and the hot chocolate chip cookies.

Introduction

Thanks for picking up, *50 Ways To Use Your Noodle*. You either have some noodles sitting around somewhere or you've seen them before and wondered, "what the heck could I use those for" (or, you just might have seen the cool cover and wanted to know what was inside). In any case, this book is packed with fun.

50 Ways to Use Your Noodle, is filled with land (or room) activities, for all ages, that can enhance the gaming potential of teachers, activity directors, program directors, experiential facilitators, parents and gatherings of all sorts. The two sections of the book include, **Games**, and **Problem-Solving Activities**.

The Games section contains activities for 2 to 30 players (and in some cases even more can play). These activities include running, jumping, dodging, chasing, tagging, ducking, swinging, and diving movements. All necessary for happy healthy bodies. We often use these games as icebreakers and warm-ups to establish a climate of fun. You will notice that some of the games are variations of traditional favorites. Adding the noodles spices them up a bit and adds a panorama of color.

The Problem Solving Activities section is designed within the spirit of Experiential Education - defined by the Association of Experiential Education as, "...a process through which a learner constructs knowledge, skill, and value from direct experience." The activities will encourage players to work together to solve a given problem, often engaging them in areas of pro-social development like teamwork, communication, conflict resolution, leadership, trust, and camaraderie.

We hope this book enriches the lives of those who play and are longing to play. We loved writing this book as much as we have loved playing all the games in it. *50 Ways To Use Your Noodle,* will provide hours of fun over and over again. Don't put this book back on the bookstore shelf, add it to yours!

The Ingredients For Fun

Noodles come in a wide variety of shapes and colors. The foam toys in this book are by no means all the noodle types the world has to offer. If you see a new noodle you like in the store and it works in the activities, use it!

Below is a list of all the foam noodle types we have utilized in some way to fit the activities in this book.

Maxaroni - A long noodle approximately 64 inches long and 3 inches in diameter

1 Maxaroni = 2 Midaronis or approximately 21 Minironis

Midaroni - Half of a Maxaroni

Minironi - A Maxaroni piece 3 inches long

Meatball - A 1 1/4 inch long Maxaroni Rex

Maxaroni Rex - A noodle approximately 58 inches long and 4 inches in diameter. Use this type of noodle for the meatballs. (Red preferably)

1 Maxaroni Rex = 46 meatballs

The ideal number of props for groups of up to 30 players:
- 30 Midaronis
- 100 Minironis
- 100 Meatballs

50 Ways To Use Your Noodle

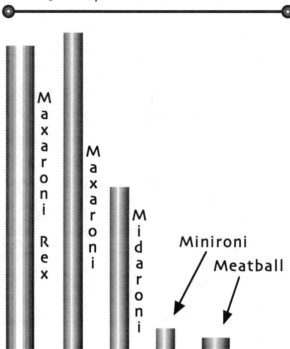

Maxaroni Rex

Maxaroni

Midaroni

Minironi

Meatball

Other materials you may want for some of the activities:

• <u>Bandannas</u> - used as blindfolds

• <u>Spot Markers</u> - usually rubber or carpet pieces used to mark the location of a player, often meatballs can be used in place of "spots"

• <u>Ropes</u> - a bright colored rope to mark boundaries

• <u>Masking Tape</u> - regular masking tape is strong enough to hold noodles together, but weak enough not to rip the foam

• <u>Clothespins</u> - wooden, spring-loaded type

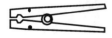

- <u>Tongs</u> - scissor-shaped type, normally used for cooking

- <u>Balls</u> - any old tennis balls or soft, tossable balls will do

- <u>Washtub</u> - metal or plastic tub

- <u>Balloons</u> - the 9-inch sizes work well

- <u>Hula-Hoops</u> - not to hula, but for boundary markers

Cutting your noodle
and other important noodle properties

You may have to cut your noodle to fit the game needs in this book, read the following pages carefully.

What you will need to cut your noodle:
• An adult
• A serrated bread knife or electric knife
• A measuring tape
• A cutting board
• A non-permanent marker

Step 1) This cutting job can be dangerous. Sharp knives cut more than foam. Be careful and never cut alone!

Step 2) Measure your noodle and mark it with a dot or small line where you want to cut it. Meatballs are one inch thick and minironis are three inches long. Midaronis are half the length of a long noodle or "maxaroni".

Step 3) Place the cutting board under your noodle before performing the noodlectomy. Failure to use a cutting board results in a sliced carpet or linoleum and a dull knife too.

Step 4) Hold the knife straight to make a perfect cut. Carefully cut through the noodle where you marked it. Continue the steps above until you finish cutting.

Step 5) Put your cutting materials away. Celebrate! It's time to play!

Other noodle properties (or The noodle howevers):
Noodles are surprisingly durable. People can stand

on them. <u>However</u>, it is best if they remove their shoes first.

Noodles can be glued together with hot glue. <u>However</u>, they will melt if the glue is too hot. Squirt some in the middle, then weld the seam. Hold the pieces together longer than usual because the foam is a heat insulator and takes longer to cool.

Noodles float in water, <u>however</u>, don't dry them by the fire or in the microwave.

Noodles are great to play with outdoors, <u>however</u>, don't leave them outside because the sun will make them brittle and faded.

Noodles look and feel great, <u>however</u>, don't try to eat one because it will give you a bad stomach ache (not to say that any stomach aches are good).

Have fun!!

Disclaimer

All active games contain some inherent risk of injury. The authors have devoted reasonable attention to the safety of any activity included within this book by describing potential hazards and playing the games themselves and with others.

The reader assumes all risk and liability for any loss or damage that may result from the use of the materials contained in this book. Liability for any claim, whether based upon errors or omissions in this book shall be limited to the purchase price of this book.

Whew! Now that that's said . . . **LET'S PLAY!**

Dressed to Play

! Games Introduction !

The Games to follow are intended to promote cooperative fun and fierce-less competition (the sort of competition where all players are having fun and are not being beaten-up by negative put-downs).

When you're getting ready to play, please consider a few things. Make sure your group is ready, both mentally and physically, for the games you are going to present. If you have a concern about the way your group will handle the noodle equipment, you might want to consider doing some other games that do not require equipment. This will give you an opportunity to observe the groups playing interaction. If you use the noodles and the group is being unsafe, please stop the activity and try something a little less threatening. If the noodle games hinder the trust development of your group, it may be harder to achieve the group development goals you may have in mind.

Make sure your group is physically ready by starting with low level movement games, followed by some stretching, and then progress into some higher level movement games. Those underused muscles tend to get noticed during the fun of noodle encounters -- use your best judgment when developing your progression of activities.

One last thought we would like to share. End the games when the players are still having fun. When you do this, groups are more likely to want to play them again in the future. This leaves your bag of games always overflowing with options.

Clap Together

GROUP SIZE:
Any size

TIME:
10 to 20 minutes

PROPS:
• Several foam meatballs for each player

OBJECTIVE:
Hold meatballs between your hands, release them
and clap, then catch the meatballs again.

SCENARIO:
Welcome to the International Sandwich Maker
Olympics! I'm Reuben Burntoast reporting to you
live from just outside the bakery window. Today's
main event is the slap & clap competition.

Contestants start with one piece of bread. The
person holds it between his hands, lets it go, claps,
and catches the bread between his hands again. After
successfully catching one slice, a contestant slaps
another piece of bread together with the first and
the slap & clap contest continues.

The rules for this competition have changed over the
years and the judges have become very watchful ever
since they caught Carl Black of Canada using
interlocking plastic bread pieces back in 1996. The
"Black Bread-Mold Incident" as it is known, changed
many of the contest's regulations. No one wants to
be in a pickle like that again.

Judges can no longer afford to loaf around with the
possibilities of deceptions. Today's competition

requires that the bread be caught only by the end pieces and in clear view of others.

World class tossers tend to linger around ten slices. Some of these contestants will not cut the mustard so stay tuned to further developments.

This is Reuben Burntoast signing off and reminding you to relish the day.

INSTRUCTIONS:
Pick up one meatball and put it in between your own hands. Now, quickly let go of the meatball, clap your hands together and catch the meatball again.

No problem? Well then, try two meatballs between your hands. Let go, clap, and catch them again. Try three, etc.

The rule is to keep your hands side by side holding the foam disks horizontally instead of one hand above the other. See how many you can hold after clapping. Fifteen meatballs is our current record.

LEADER NOTES:
This game requires eye-hand coordination. The fun aspect of the game happens when you clap and try to grab the meatballs only to have them squirt out in an explosion of foam.

VARIATIONS:
Try to clap twice before catching the meatballs.
Try a mixture of minironis and meatballs.
Toss a horizontal stack of meatballs for a partner to catch.

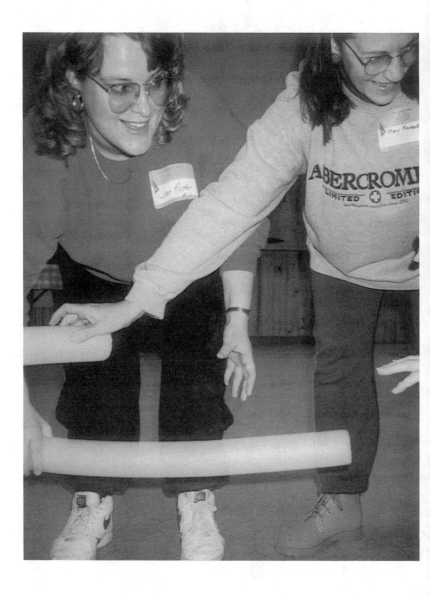

Pass The Pasta

GROUP SIZE:
10 to 20 players (maybe more if you're into
adventure)

TIME:
10 to 20 minutes

PROPS:
• 6 Midaronis

We like to use two sets of colors, like three reds and
three yellows (if the group gets up to three each).
The total number will depend on the size of the
group and the challenge they want to meet.

OBJECTIVE:
Pass the pasta without getting completely confused.

HISTORY:
Pass The Pasta is a cousin to the game Watch It.
Who knows, maybe someday the two games will get
together for total chaos.

INSTRUCTIONS:
So far we have found it best to have even numbers of
players for this one (but this is not set in stone --
remember -- be creative and then tell us how it
works!). You can add or subtract yourself to make
the numbers playable.

Have the group standing in a close circle. There
should be a few inches between each player's
shoulders (adjust the spacing if you need to make it
better for your group). Count off by one and twos or
apples and bananas. I'll do one of our typical sessions
verbatim assuming I'm in the game...

"Being an apple, what I would like to do is get this apple pasta (red midaroni) all the way around the circle back to me. But I only want the apple pasta passed to the apples. Holding the pasta in my right hand, I want to pass it to the apple to my right, but first I have to say, 'WATCH IT' (with feeling) to the banana right next to me so I don't bruise him. (Demonstrate the pass going in front of the banana player across his legs.) The next apple takes the pasta with her right hand then repeats the motion going over to the next apple to the right. Don't forget to say, 'WATCH IT!" Keep this going around nice and slow until the pasta returns to me. Remember, we don't want any bruised fruit here. Great! Now we'll have the bananas try it. (Give a yellow midaroni to the player on your right -- I stash the noodles behind me so I can add and subtract as the game goes on.) Same deal. Right hand grasp, 'WATCH IT' to the apple on your right, next banana passes the pasta to the next banana. Go all the way around nice and slow so you get the idea. Now let's add a bit of a challenge. I'll start the apple pasta going, then I'll tell my neighbor banana to get the banana pasta going. What's going to happen? You might be right; let's find out."

You see the idea. Start out slowly so the players get the hang of it, then add as much challenge as they can handle. Don't forget about safety during all the fun. If it becomes too wild, take out noodles as they get to you. No Bruises!!

Swattin' Flies

GROUP SIZE:
9 to 12 players

TIME:
2 to 4 minutes each round

PROPS:
- 3 Midaronis
- 40 Minironis (lots make it fun)
- A nice big tub
- Spot marker for each player

PREPARATION:
The large tub will be the center point of the set up.
Place a spot marker on the ground for each player 10
feet away from the tub (e.g., if there were 12 players,
the spot markers would be around the tub like the

hours marked around a clock). Place all the minironis around the outside of the spot markers.

OBJECTIVE:
The Swatters try to prevent the flies from entering the tub.

INSTRUCTIONS:
Have each player choose a spot marker to stand on while explaining the game. Choose 3 volunteers to work together as Swatters. Give them each a midaroni and ask them to stand near the tub.

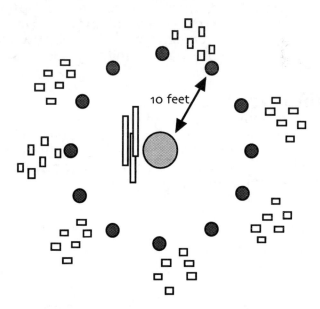

10 feet

The players standing on the spot markers will be Flyers. Their objective will be to toss as many flies (minironis) into the tub within the allotted amount of time. They are only allowed to toss flies while standing on a spot marker. The spot markers may not be moved. When a player is touching a spot, she is safe from any swats. If swatted while off of the spot, she must stand frozen for 20 seconds (counting out loud) before reflying flies.

The three Swatters near the tub will be trying to keep the flies out of the tub by swatting the flies with the noodle (not any other body part). Swatters cannot move or manipulate the tub in any way. Swatters may swat Flyers who are off of the spots. Be careful not to swat above the shoulders.

Set a time for each round. We find 2 to 3 minutes is a good range. However, some groups can go longer if they are still having fun with it. If you or the group chooses to, count the number of flies in the tub after the allotted time. Compare this to other groups of three to determine the top Swatters. (We always encourage healthy competition -- if it is done without putting down any other player in the group, it is healthy.)

LEADER NOTES:
Make sure your group is ready for this activity. Be aware of Hyper Swatters. These are the ones with a bit too much energy that might swat another player too hard. Stop play any time there is a potential for an unsafe environment.

Pass It To

GROUP SIZE:
8 to 12 players

TIME:
4 to 6 minutes

PROPS:
• 1 Midaroni

OBJECTIVE:
Learn the names of the other players in the group, and get out of the center of the circle.

HISTORY:
This is a great historical game by Karl Rohnke . . . made famous by activity nuts around the world.

INSTRUCTIONS:

Form a circle of players sitting down facing the center with their knees up and their feet flat on the ground. The playing space is the area outlined by the player's feet. This area should be about 8 to 10 feet in diameter (as you play this game you can adjust the space to the desired challenge).

As instructors, we start out in the middle of the circle of feet, with the midaroni, to explain the directions.

Choose one of the sitting players to start. Have this player say, "I pass it to Sally" (Sally being one of the players in the circle). The action starts here. The center player wants to first locate Sally and then tag Sally below the knees with the noodle before Sally can say, "I pass it to . . . (some other player's name)." If Sally passes it to, "Bill" (for instance), the center player must first locate Bill and try for the tag before Bill passes it to . . .

If a tag is made before the pass, the sitting player stands up in the center and the center player sits down in the circle, knees up and feet flat on the ground. Then, the player that just sat down (the one that was just in the center) starts the action. He says, "I pass it to, Sam!" and the game goes on.

One other proviso: If a sitting player happens to flinch (any movement to avoid being tagged), that player is IN THE CENTER!

LEADER NOTES:

We always get involved in this game since it can be supervised while playing. If the center player is in for a while, condense the playing area and restart. If this player continues to struggle, have him switch out with another player sitting down.

Doctor Tag

GROUP SIZE:
15 to 30+ players

TIME:
5 to 15 minutes

PROPS:
• Approximately one midaroni noodle for every ten players

OBJECTIVE:
Avoid being tagged, but if you are tagged, you can be cured with a shot from the doctor.

HISTORY:
Tag games are some of the most physical and exciting

games played by kids of all ages. This tag game takes full advantage of the properties of the foam noodle. People like to playfully strike others with the foam and fortunately it doesn't hurt. We think this game will be a hit.

PREPARATION:
Identify the play area boundaries and mark or define them to the group.

SCENARIO:
An aggressive infection has spread throughout the hospital. It seems that someone was picking her nose while someone else coughed without covering his mouth and now the combination of germs has mutated into a disaster.

All the patients have an unstoppable urge to spread the germs by touching other people. If a patient touches you, cover the germs with your hand and get to the doctor for a shot. If you get touched three times before getting a shot, you will die a dramatic death.

Your only hope is a cure from a doctor who must hit your hand with the foam syringe. The doctor may have to give you two shots for a complete cure.

If you infect (tag) a doctor, she becomes a patient and you become the new doctor.

If more than four patients die, the hospital will be shut down and the doctor will have to pay her malpractice insurance deductibles.

INSTRUCTIONS:
This is a tag game designed to give everyone a fighting chance of extended life.

There are two roles: Doctors and patients.

The patients try to tag each other and the doctor(s). A tag to another patient means that the tagged patient holds the place where he was tagged. A second tag to the same patient means that he also holds the second place where he was tagged. A third tag to the same patient means he dies a horrible death and lies on the ground.

Meanwhile, the doctor(s) tries to cure the patients of their wounds by hitting them with the foam noodle on the hand covering their wound. When a doctor hits a wound, it is cured. Unfortunately, if a doctor is tagged, she becomes a patient and the patient gets the foam noodle and becomes a doctor.

When everyone understands the rules, the leader shouts "911", and the game begins.

The game ends when four or more patients have died.

LEADER NOTES:
If you have enough midaronis, allow for one doctor for every ten patients.

Some people can get rough playing the game. You may need to add safety instructions such as: No tagging above the shoulders. You may not tag anyone with your head or feet. Race-walk, don't run (optional).

Join the fun if you are the leader. This game is a great way for you to model good behavior and have fun at the same time.

VARIATIONS:
Add a circled boundary to the play area for the doctors to stay in. The doctors can see patients who come into the circle (hospital) but stay safe from the germs. This is an easy way to include people who are unable to run.

Partner Tag

GROUP SIZE:
4 to 30+ players

TIME:
60 to 90 seconds a round

PROPS:
• 1 Midaroni for every two players

PREPARATION:
Setting boundaries will be the instructor's prerogative. The smaller the boundaries, the quicker the game will be. Smaller boundaries, however, allow less open space to move around in. Larger boundaries allow for more open space to move, but require a larger aerobic capacity.

HISTORY:
Partner Tag is a variation of a game from Karl Rohnke. We added the noodles for aesthetic appeal.

INSTRUCTIONS:
Have players pair up with someone in the group. If there is an odd number, the instructor will get to play. You can play with groups of three if the instructor needs to assume another role during the game. Ask someone from each pair to obtain one noodle.

First determine the boundary area and share this with all the pairs of players. The objective, when the game begins, is for the partner with the noodle to tag her partner. That's it . . . with just a couple of provisos.

Tags with the noodles must be below the knees. After making the tag, the tagger drops the noodle near the feet of the taggee (the tagger does not throw the noodle into the outskirts of town). When a player is tagged by her partner, she must do a 360 degree spin, then pick up the noodle to pursue her partner for the tag-back. Repeat above until the game clock expires.

BE AWARE! The playing area will be obstructed with other bodies, so the speed of the game should be kept to a fast walk.

Set the game clock for the first round to 60 seconds and see how the players hold out. If this turns out to be too short, extend the time for the next rounds. Take a good breather between rounds -- they'll need it.

LEADER NOTES:
We find, especially with younger groups, the speed factor is a concern -- even with the fast walking rule.

To slow the action down, add a "key". We use the meatballs (if you want to start out with this option, play Flippin' Burgers before Partner Tag to get a little practice). The key (meatball) keeps the motor going when it is on the back of a player's hand (no holding it on there either). As long as the key is there, the player may move. If it falls off, the player must stop and replace the key before moving again. This rule goes for all players during the game.

There is a heightened potential for "head butts" here. So keep reminding the players to "WATCH OUT" for others!

VARIATIONS:
Players stand with their partner and link up. Match the pair with another pair; now two linked players chase the other two linked players. The linked pair who will chase first, has 2 midaronis. The chasers have both of the noodles until a tag occurs, then the noodles are dropped then retrieved by the new chasers. Remember to spin around 360 degrees before pursuing.

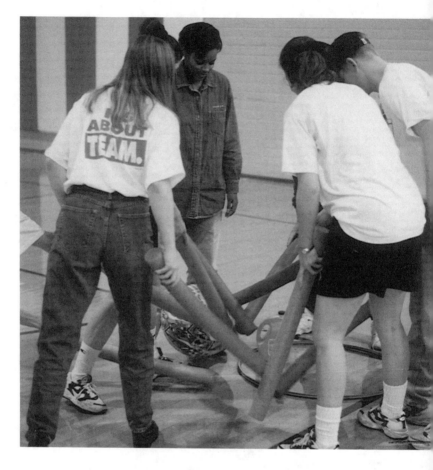

Noodle Hockey

GROUP SIZE:
8 to 16 players

TIME:
Four 5-minute quarters or three 6-minute periods (depending on how close you want to stay to the "real" game)

PROPS:
- 1 Midaroni for each player
- 1 Red playground ball (slightly deflated if possible)
- 2 Hula-Hoops
- 2 Empty gallon water jugs.

PREPARATION:
Set down the two hula-hoops about 50 feet apart and place a plastic jug upright in the center of the hoop. (Athletic cups for both genders are optional.)

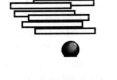

OBJECTIVE:
Teams work together to try and score as many points as possible within regulation time.

HISTORY:
This adaptation of the icy game was one of Chris' first activities with the noodles. It turned out to be so much fun he had to think of more. So, the birth of a book took place.

INSTRUCTIONS:

Creatively divide the group in half. (Please avoid the, "best-players-are-captains-and-pick-everyone-until-someone-is-last-and-feels-bad" division. We sure would appreciate it.) For simplicity, try to give each team different colored noodles. Each player gets one noodle.

If you need to limit boundaries with lines, tell the group where the boundaries are before starting. Since teams tend to want to score a goal, the ball usually does not stray too far away. If it does get too far off, just stop play and do a roll-off (we'll tell you later).

One point is scored when the ball hits the bottle inside the hoop. If the ball knocks over the bottle, it is two points. Scores can happen from any area around the hoop. Players are not allowed inside the hoop area. If a defending player moves the hoop and causes the bottle to tip over, it is two points for the opposing team. If the offensive team moves the hoop and knocks down the bottle, no points are scored and a roll-off occurs at the center of the field. After any points are scored, a center roll-off takes place.

Each team will start out on one side of the designated center line. Two players will face each other for the "roll-off" start. The instructor/ref. stands away to the side of the two center players (You will want to stand away to the side!), then rolls the ball between the two to start play.

Noodles may only be held by one end and neither hand can hold the noodle past the midway point of that noodle. All swings must stay below the waist. Any swings above the waist will result in a 60-second penalty (assign a designated area for players to stand during this time). At no time are players allowed to use any body part to move the ball. If this happens, there is a 60-second penalty.

There are really no goalies in this game, but we do let one person stand around by the hoop if the teams agree to this.

LEADER NOTES:
It will be very important to keep a close eye out for safety violations. This game is a lot of fun when all players are following the rules. Don't let anything slide.

About the "goalie" issue, encourage (sometimes we do make) the teams to change goalies often. Share the responsibility of this stressful position.

Flippin' Burgers

GROUP SIZE:
2 to 30+

TIME:
2 to 3 minutes a round

PROPS:
- 1 Midaroni for each player
- 1 Meatball for each player

OBJECTIVE:
Each player tries to flip the meatball, or in this case the burger, off of any other player's hand and keeps his own from being flipped.

HISTORY:
Mike Spiller introduced us to a very similar game called "Knock Off". In his version you place a small rock, chip, or washer on one hand and try to knock off the other player's rock with the same hand.

SCENARIO:
You are all Burgermeisters in for the international furious flipping frenzy competition. You and your burger buddies gather in the grease pit to see who will be the master burgermeister. After a few warm up rounds of non-elimination, the real game begins. Who will be the meister with the last burger?

INSTRUCTIONS:
Equip each player with props. Players can choose to hold the minironi by one of the ends in either hand. The meatball will be placed on the back of the other hand so it doesn't fall off (yet). There will be some skill involved, so do a bit of practicing moving around keeping the meatball balanced.

Set up a good-sized boundary area for your group. Let there be enough room to move around safely.

We like to play several rounds of about 2 to 3 minutes each. Burgers go flying pretty quick, so it might take even less time.

All players are playing against each other. Their objective is to flip off the burgers of other players without loosing their own burger.

At no time during the round can players hold their burger to the back of their hand with any type of resource. Players must also keep their hands off the floor (mostly for safety reasons).

Players must keep their burgers and hits with the minironi below shoulder level.

LEADER NOTES:
This game tends to be a lot of fun if presented properly. Talk up the challenge but don't emphasize winners and losers. We often play a bunch of rounds. If a player's burger falls off, just pick it up and get into the game. After each round, ask if any player has discovered some good tricks to keep the burger on his hand or some great moves to flip the burger off someone else's hand. We play enough rounds to give all players a chance to find success, then we go into the ultra (dare I say) competitive FB. If players lose their burger, they move outside of the boundaries. However, they can still flip off burgers if any of the active players gets close enough to them (good boundary lines are helpful). Rounds go pretty fast, so there is not much waiting around for a new game to start.

Hittin' It

GROUP SIZE:
2 to 16 players

TIME:
10 to 15 minutes

PROPS:
- 2 Meatballs for each player
- 1 Minironi for each player

OBJECTIVE:
Players keep the minironis active as long as possible.

INSTRUCTIONS:
Each player will hold the meatballs flat against the palms of his hands. These are now paddle-type instruments.

Players start out individually by picking up their minironi, giving it a toss, then trying to keep it up in the air by batting it with the meatballs. The irregular shape of the mini makes this task somewhat challenging.

After a few minutes of practice, pair up players. Using one mini, bat it back and forth keeping it moving as long as possible. Have pairs count the number of hits they can obtain before the mini hits the ground. One player may not hit the mini more than two times in a row.

Once each pair has a chance to sharpen their skills, match up two pairs to make small groups of four. Use one mini. Count hits within the group. Ask them to try and improve their score as their skills get better. We have also found that letting players share their learnings with each other during the process develops an enhanced team spirit.

After four, go to eight. From eight, to sixteen. Whatever splits work the best for the group. When one group remains, talk about the more effective strategies players have discovered. Then, as one, try to establish the ultimate Hittin' It world record (for that group).

LEADER NOTES:
We like to emphasize GBs (Group Bests). Comparing your group to other groups may not be the best way to build group uniqueness. There are times, however, that "motivational comparison" is used. Just remember to keep in mind the dynamics of your players and use your best judgment.

Delta Tag

GROUP SIZE:
4 to 30+ players

TIME:
5 to 10 minutes

PROPS:
• 1 Midaroni for every four players.

OBJECTIVE:
A lone tagger tries to noodle tag one of the other members of the group while being guarded by the other two members of the group.

HISTORY:
Here is another great game from our friend Karl Rohnke. We added the noodle to make the game a bit easier for us old folks.

INSTRUCTIONS:
Gather together in groups of four -- explore creative ways to put groups together if they need a little help. Have one of the players in the group get a midaroni noodle.

The player with the noodle will be designated as the first tagger. The other three players hold hands forming a triangle shape. Have one of the players in the triangle shape volunteer to be the taggee for the first game.

The starting formation will have the tagger, armed with a noodle, looking at the taggee through the two other players. What do these other two players do? They are the blockers. They try to prevent the tagger from tagging the taggee by moving and turning together, all the while holding hands. The tagger is not allowed to go under the blockers.

The tagger may tag the taggee only below the waist. If this happens, the taggee becomes the tagger, the tagger becomes a blocker, and one of the blockers is the new taggee. Then continue the game.

LEADER NOTES:
If a tagger in one of the groups has difficulty tagging the taggee, ask them to switch roles. Make sure everyone has the chance to play in each role, and no player is stuck in the same role too long.

50 Ways To Use Your Noodle

Circle Drop

GROUP SIZE:
5 to 20 players

TIME:
10 to 20 minutes

PROPS:
• One midaroni for each player

OBJECTIVE:
Try not to drop the noodles while you exchange them with the other players.

HISTORY:
This activity comes from a field hockey drill that teaches coordination, concentration and speed. Theresa Ostrander introduced us to the activity.

INSTRUCTIONS:
Take a noodle and stand in a circle with a couple of feet between each person. Place one end of your noodle on the ground and hold the noodle vertically by the other end.

Now we are going to do several things to practice coordination, concentration, speed, and teamwork. At each step we will practice enough to stay in control of the noodles, then move on to fancier moves. Try to keep the noodles from falling over.

- Let go of your noodle, clap your hands, hold the noodle again
- Let go, clap twice, catch the noodle
- Let go, turn around, catch the noodle
- Let go, move to the right one position, catch the noodle
- Let go, move to the left one position, catch the noodle
- Let go, move to the right two positions, catch the noodle
- Count off around the circle. All the odds go to the left one position, evens go to the right one position
- All the odds go to the left two positions, evens go to the right two positions
- Lift your noodle, bounce it on the floor, move to the right one position, catch the noodle

LEADER NOTES:
This is one of those activities that can go too long if you are not careful. Make sure people are having fun. Any size group can do the activity, but groups over twenty people may have a harder time all completing a step without a noodle falling.

If the noodles seem to stand on their own it certainly reduces the challenge. Ask the whole group to put their hands on their midaroni and push down about 8 inches. Bending the noodles tips them off balance.

By no means should you expect every group to complete all of the steps listed above. The steps are listed to give you an idea of what might be fun to increase the challenge.

If you are outside, a breeze can make the activity much more difficult.

VARIATIONS:
Try it while each person holds a noodle in the air.
Try it with the noodle resting on a table.

50 Ways To Use Your Noodle

Hamburger Press

GROUP SIZE:
2 players per Hamburger Press

TIME:
About 3 to 5 minutes for one attempt

PROPS:
- At least 30 meatballs (however, some players may need more)

OBJECTIVE:
Pairs of players try to press as many meatballs as possible together horizontally between their hands.

INSTRUCTIONS:
Dump out at least 30 meatballs (or more if you have them) in a big pile.

Each player will use one hand as the press, and the other as an adder. Players start by pressing the palms of their press hands together. Then, using their adding hands, add one meatball at a time between the pressed hands. If they want to keep track, they should count as they go cause if they lose-um, all the hamburgers get mixed up with the others on the floor.

Count any burgers that were in the press before the FFWWAAPP of burgers occurs. What is the FFWWAAPP? You'll see!

LEADER NOTES:
We like to stress this game as a challenge to the pairs, not a competition between pairs. Go PBs. (Paired Best).

Chopper

GROUP SIZE:
5 to 15 players

TIME:
10 to 20 minutes

PROPS:
- 1 Midaroni
- 2 Ropes (optional)

OBJECTIVE:
Avoid being hit by the foam sword while passing the sword handler.

HISTORY:
In the endless search for uses of foam noodles, camp leaders at Camp Lutherhoma near Tahlequah, Oklahoma created Chopper for their campers. It was a big hit (pun intended).

PREPARATION:
Make a narrow runway. Lay the two ropes parallel to each other on the ground approximately 4 feet apart and 10 feet long. You can eliminate the ropes if you play on a sidewalk and use the walkway as the boundary.

SCENARIO:
While you and some friends were on your way to play miniature golf a strange feeling came over you all. As you entered the course, people looked at you strangely. All of a sudden you realized that you had turned into golf balls. The dimples on your cheeks and the cheeks of the rest of the group were unmistakable.

You still wanted to play a game of miniature golf, so you decided to go for it. It was strange at first. Not having to use a putter, you just rolled (ran) straight toward each cup and made several holes-in-one!

Everything was going so well until the 18th hole. Between you and the cup stood a mighty warrior who swung his sword so that it cut through your path. The warrior just stood there swinging over and over in the same way. You noticed that you could make it if you timed it just right. Can you avoid the sword and make it safely to the other side?

INSTRUCTIONS:

When the game begins, each person will take a turn standing in the alley between the ropes while swinging his sword. As the sword slices through the air, the rest of the players will attempt to pass the swinging sword while staying within the boundaries and not being hit.

Ask everyone to think of a movement to make with a foam sword and practice it.

The one challenge is that the sword holder must repeat his or her one movement without changing the swing or the timing of the swing. The sword holder's feet may move as long as the steps are repeated. It may look like a strange dance movement.

The people passing the sword holder should go one at a time and not touch the sword holder or the sword. If the sword touches a player or the player steps out of bounds, that player is out until everyone has had a chance to attempt a pass and the next sword holder starts.

The sword holder is trying to make a repetitive swinging pattern that will hit the most people. The rest of the players are trying their best to avoid being hit.

When everyone has had a chance to swing the sword, try the game again to see what strategies change.

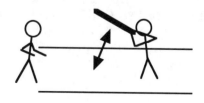

LEADER NOTES:

For this activity the sword holder's position is important. We find it valuable to demonstrate one round to model the appropriate actions of the chopper. If the players include children, an adult can be the first sword holder and demonstrate the type of swings that are fair. Fast movements are okay; however, they must be repeated over and over in the same way.

When people play this game they often have the same feelings as when they enter into a jump rope game. The concept is similar except that the rope has a brain and can do much more than go in circles.

VARIATIONS:

Widen or narrow the boundaries.
Blindfold the sword holder.
Have the sword holder turn his or her back to the group.
Add several sword holders in the alley, each with a different swinging motion.

Balloon Bash

GROUP SIZE:
6 to 16 players

TIME:
10 to 20 minutes a game split into quarters or halves

PROPS:
• 1 Midaroni for each player.

PREPARATION:
To go through fewer balloons, we recommend that you play this one indoors. However, see VARIATIONS for the outdoor version. You will need to choose a center line, and two end lines equally distant from the center line (a basketball court is ideal).

OBJECTIVE:
Teams try to move a balloon across their opponent's back line for points.

HISTORY:
Karl Rohnke shares yet another game with us. His favorite version is One-On-One, Mono-a-Mono. He does suggest a team version that we share with you.

INSTRUCTIONS:
Creatively divide the team in half. Give each player a noodle. It is helpful for team members to have like-colored noodles. Teams line up on the end line they plan to defend. One player from each team starts at the center line for the drop-off. After the two center players slap their midaronis on the ground three times together, the ref. drops the balloon down in-between them to start play. Once the balloon is in play, all players are free to move around the playing field.

Teams play to knock the balloon past the end line of their opposing team. The balloon must also make contact with the floor behind the line in order to count as a point. When a point is scored, the balloon comes back out to the center for another drop-off.

Only the noodle may come in contact with the

balloon. Any other incidental contact with the balloon will result in a half-court foul. A half-court foul is called by the referee. The player who is fouled must proceed immediately across the center line to the other half of the playing area. This player must stay there until the balloon crosses back over the center line. Then he can get involved in the action again.

At no time may a player strike another player above the waist with a noodle. If this occurs, a half-court foul is called. There will be incidental contact allowed below the waist, but only during balloon bashing. Any purposeful human contact with the noodles will result in removal from the game for a time to be determined by the referee.

LEADER NOTES:
We choose to play this game with groups we feel can handle the safety considerations of this game. The game isn't fun any more if someone gets hurt.

VARIATIONS:
If you want to try this one outside, you might want to consider a few factors. Tennis courts are great playing areas. However, please remove the net posts! The wind has a lot of fun with balloons, and the grass likes to pop them. We have played in the grass on still days and if the balloon pops on the ground, it is one point against the defending side of that ground. If the balloon crosses the back line and pops (or doesn't pop) on the ground, it is two points for the offensive team.

Balloon Volleyball

GROUP SIZE:
8 to 16 players

TIME:
20 to 30 minutes a game

PROPS:
- 1 Midaroni for each player
- A few large balloons (the larger the better -- the helium type balloons we find are the best).
- If you want to play the ultra variation, 2 hula-hoops are needed.

PREPARATION:
You will need a horizontal line approximately eight feet from the ground -- a volleyball net is ideal. A long rope strung between two points also works well. You may want to shorten up the standard volleyball back line for smaller groups. As you play you can adjust accordingly.

OBJECTIVE:
Teams work together to score points to ultimately win a game.

INSTRUCTIONS:
This game is a fun variation of standard volleyball, with a few changes.

Divide the group into two equal teams. Give each player a noodle and then have teams stand on opposite sides of the horizontal line or net. Give a large inflated balloon to one of the teams. This balloon must start behind the designated back line. (For a little faster action, try adding some water to the balloon -- the float potential goes down the more water you use.)

The balloon may be touched only by the noodles. The noodle must be hit by at least four different players, and no more than six hits before it goes over the net. To put the balloon in play, the server, standing behind the end line, tosses the balloon in the air, then hits the balloon with the noodle. Now the team has at least three more hits to get the balloon over the net.

55

The serving team scores a point if the opposing team violates the "hits rule" or if the balloon touches the ground on the opposing team's side. The serve changes sides when the serving team violates the hits rule or the balloon touches the ground on the serving team's side. Setting a game winning score will be up to the skill level of the group. We find the younger groups need a higher game score and the older groups can have lengthy games with a lower game score.

LEADER NOTES:
This game has been great for cross-drill-training for volleyball teams. Balloon volleyball requires a great deal of communication between team members if they plan to be successful.

We didn't mention any specifics on holding the noodle. There have been some interesting methods used. The one thing we have asked the players is not to bend the noodles during the game.

There have been some groups that have asked for two noodles for each player. Our experience has proven this to be manageable with smaller groups and not so good with larger groups -- but hey, we never listened to our mothers when they gave us advice!?

If you play this game outdoors, any pop of the balloon results in a point against the team it popped on.

VARIATIONS:
Ultra balloon volleyball includes hula-hoops. A hoop is placed near the back line of each team's side. One player from each team must stand in the hoop. Whenever the balloon is on a team's side, the hoop player must make a hit on the balloon before it goes back over to the other team's side. If this player does

not make a hit on the balloon, it results in a point for the other team or loss of serve. Rotate a new player into the hoop each time the serve changes.

Live Wire

GROUP SIZE:
12 to 30+ players

TIME:
10 to 15 minutes a game

PROPS:
• 2 Midaronis

OBJECTIVE:
Each player tries to avoid the live wire so he or she is the last person remaining.

HISTORY:
Here is another game from the tome of Karl Rohnke. Karl's history of fun goes back to his younger days when he melted "live" ammunition on his mother's kitchen stove. (He didn't know it was live until too

late.) I'm glad he survived to share this game with us.

INSTRUCTIONS:
Ask for a pair of players to volunteer to be the "Live Wire." Give each player in the pair a noodle.

Set the boundaries large enough for some safe running and small enough for a challenge (you'll figure it out).

The live wire pair will be moving together to tag roaming players. Tags are done with the noodles any safe place on the body (you may have to define "safe place" for some groups). When tagged, the player joins the live wire end, taking the noodle to become the new tagger for the live wire. There are now three players connected together. These three go off to find another person to tag. The game continues in this fashion until there is only two roaming players remaining. These players become the live wire for the next game (that is if the group wants to play another round).

LEADER NOTES:
If you have a really large group and the live wire becomes too large to manage, grab a couple more midaronis and split the line in the middle, giving the noodles to the new ends.

Some groups may also need a little safety talk about hand holding and pulling arms out of sockets. If it cannot be safe, please don't play it.

VARIATIONS:
Start with all players connected in pairs. Choose one pair to be the live wire. When a roaming pair is tagged, they go to each end of the live wire.

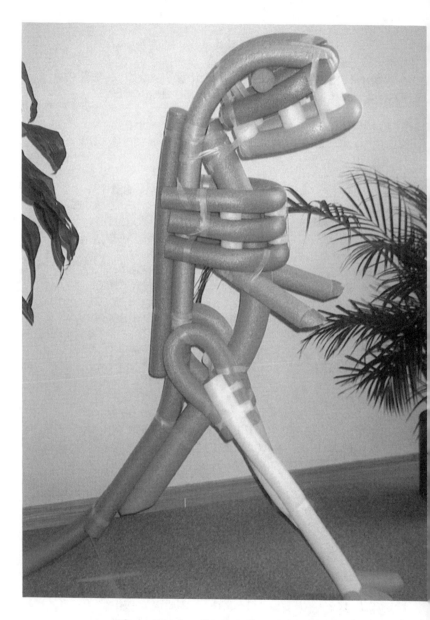

The Rare "Maxaroni Rex"

Structures

GROUP SIZE:
1 to 5 players

TIME:
15 minutes to 1 hour

PROPS:
- A variety of noodle pieces, shapes, and colors.
- Glue, tape, or toothpicks (optional)

OBJECTIVE:
Build anything using pieces of noodles.

HISTORY:
As kids, we all enjoyed building with blocks or rocks or anything else that stacked. Structures provides the material to fulfill that need.

PREPARATION:
Gather any used or new noodles and cut them into a variety of shapes and lengths.

SCENARIO:
Professor Jones has come to you for help concerning the latest archeological find in South Africa. It seems that he has discovered an ancient city where both humans and dinosaurs lived together. The professor has even found some bones of the enormous Maxaroni Rex.

Your job is to create a model of the city and its inhabitants.

INSTRUCTIONS:
Because of the risk of stifling someone's imagination, the instructions for this activity are only as specific as you make them.

Have fun. Be creative. Think of a theme and build it.

LEADER NOTES:
Some people need a little spark to get their
imagination going. The following are some themes
that might start someone building a masterpiece:
Oriental garden, amusement park, underwater
world, new animal, vehicle of the future, my family,
mountain home, factory, bird house.

50 Ways To Use Your Noodle

Noodle Doodles

GROUP SIZE:
1 to 10 players

TIME:
15 to 45 minutes

PROPS:
• Maxaronis, midaronis, minironis, and meatballs

OBJECTIVE:
Lay noodles different ways to represent a scene or a word.

PREPARATION:
Select a story like the scenario below or a set of words for the participants to doodle.

SCENARIO:
Once upon a time, there lived a little _____ in a beautiful mountain village near _____. The little _____ was always playing in the _____ and resting in the sun while cool summer breezes blew across the _____.

One day a _____ came to the village to pose a _____ to the town's people. "I have the answers to all your _____ problems," the _____ said. "Of course my price will be high and you will have to pay me in _____."

The villagers were _____ about their new situation until the little _____ came up with a way to handle the circumstance. All we have to do is give the _____ some _____ and the _____ will never _____ again. The whole mountain village _____ and everyone _____ happily for ever and ever.

INSTRUCTIONS:
You will be building pictures or spelling words with the foam noodles.

As I read a word or if a picture pops into your head, quickly lay it out in a noodle drawing on the floor. Feel free to be creative. If, for example, I say "house", you all would quickly design and build a house with the noodles.

The idea is to use the floor like a sheet of paper and the noodles as the pen.

LEADER NOTES:
Noodle Doodles works well as a fast paced game or as a leisurely art project. Depending on how many noodle pieces you have, the doodles can be fairly extravagant.

You can use the scenario above with two teams at

once who try to make a picture or spell a word while a person watches and says which doodle she can understand first.

VARIATIONS:
Try a group contest where everyone spells an answer with noodles.

Old One Tooth

GROUP SIZE:
8 to 15 players per snake

TIME:
10 to 15 minutes

PROPS:
• 1 Midaroni

OBJECTIVE:
Tag the person at the end of the line with a noodle.

HISTORY:
The first time I played a game similar to this one, it was called Catch The Dragon's Tail from the New Games Book. Everyone ran so hard that we couldn't catch our breath for quite a while and a friend almost lost his shorts. It is tough to laugh when you are breathing so hard.

PREPARATION:
Pick a level playing surface with no holes or things to trip over.

SCENARIO:
Old "One Tooth" was one of the oldest snakes to have ever lived in Texas. He got the name One Tooth because of his one fang that jutted out the front of his mouth. History has it that he bit a rock in his younger years and the rock broke one of his fangs and straightened the other. It was around that time that One Tooth discovered he was nearsighted.

Normally vision is a vital sense to have in the wilderness, but old One Tooth lived to be old because of his quick reflexes and his "strike first and ask questions later" policy. Unfortunately, he has often mistaken his own tail for a meal.

INSTRUCTIONS:
This game is going to require you to be in one line holding on to each other. The person in the front of the line will hold a noodle.

The last person in the line will be trying to avoid being hit by the noodle at the front of the line.

Line up in groups of six to twelve people and hold on to the waist of the person in front of you. When I say "GO", the front person in the line will try to tag the back of the last person in line. If the line disconnects, everyone should stop and we'll start again connected.

When the back-side of the player at the end of the line is tagged, we'll stop to let the front person go to the end of the line and the next person in front will get the noodle to try the game again.

LEADER NOTES:
This game requires a lot of energy from the players. Be prepared to stop the game if it is getting too rough for someone. Don't allow people to stick their fingers in belt loops because of the potential for hurting fingers or breaking belt loops. Holding on to the back of someone's pants is not a good idea either. Pants tend to rip under the pressure; or worse yet, there is wedgie potential.

VARIATIONS:
Play in several lines with each line tagging itself or other lines.
Try lining up holding hands, but be careful of cracking the whip.

Bustin' Burgers

GROUP SIZE:
2 players (A bunch of pairs can play at the same time.)

TIME:
As long as interest is available

PROPS:
- 1 Midaroni
- 6 Meatballs for each pair

OBJECTIVE:
One player tries to "Bust" (just figuratively) as many meatballs out of the air with a midaroni before the meat hits the ground.

HISTORY:
As we were brainstorming ideas for this book, all this talk about food led to the good old food fight days of traditional education. Someone mentioned that she used to protect herself with the tray and even batted food items back at tossers. One thing led to another and now we have Bustin' Burgers.

INSTRUCTIONS:
Designate the Launcher and the Buster within each pair. The Launcher gets the meatballs and the Buster, the noodle.

The Launcher stands about 6 to 8 feet in front of the Buster as in a pitcher-batter formation in baseball. Have pairs try a little one-burger. The Launcher flies (like a Frisbee) the simulated patty towards the Buster. The Buster, with a one-handed midaroni swing, tries to hit the meatball. Any touch of the meatball is a hit in this game.

After some practice, and taking some turns at the one-burger, try the two-burger. The Launcher tosses both patties at once (put one patty on top of the other and toss it in with one hand). In most cases, the patties split apart in flight so the Buster has to work a bit to hit both burgers.

The long term goal here is to see how many patties can be flung (a trick in itself), and then how many patties the buster can hit before they all fall to the ground. (So far we think the record is 3.)

LEADER NOTES:
If you anticipate any safety problems, adjust any of the guidelines to fit your setting.

Sometimes we will have the Launcher stand to the side (like down the third base line) so the Buster hits the burgers out into an open space. However, you really don't know where those patties will go!?

Clothespin Samurai

GROUP SIZE:
5 to 12 players

TIME:
20 to 30 minutes

PROPS:
- 1 Midaroni
- 20 or more clothespins
- Enough spots, markers, or meatballs for all but one player
- 1 Bandanna

OBJECTIVE:
A blind samurai attempts to strike the other players before they remove the clothespins from his clothing.

HISTORY:
In preparation for this book we asked several people to think of games using foam noodles. Renny Cavener created this game of quickness and strategy.

SCENARIO:
The ancient samurai depended on all of their senses to fight for and protect the emperor. As a way of enhancing their skills, they played a game. A group of samurai would clip bells to the clothing of a blindfolded samurai. The remaining swordsmen would surround him and attempt to steal his bells without being hit with a stick.

They say that the blindfolded warrior could sense the movements of the other players. Fortunately, the sighted samurai were skilled at moving without being heard. Everyone strengthened their skills.

INSTRUCTIONS:

The game we are about to play involves two types of people. One person in the middle of the circle will try to hit people with a foam noodle before they can steal clothespins clipped to her clothing. The people on the edge of the circle will avoid being hit by the noodle while they go for one of the clothespins on the person in the middle.

Stand in a circle that is at least fifteen feet across with a spot marker in hand. Place your marker on the ground at your feet, then stand on the marker. Everyone on the edge of the circle is "safe" as long as they are standing on their marker. No one may move any of the markers. The player with the sword will need approximately 20 clothespins attached to her clothing. The people on the outside edge of the circle start off with no clothespins.

One player will blindly stand in the middle of the circle with a foam sword. When she thinks someone is off a marker and trying to get a clothespin, she can swing the sword to hit the person.

If the person who is hit has a clothespin, that person must drop the clothespin at the feet of the samurai and return to his spot before going for another clothespin. However, if the person is hit and does not have a clothespin, then he must return to his spot marker and count to out loud to 30 before playing again.

When anyone on the outside circle gets three clothespins, that person becomes the new samurai and the old samurai must give up all her clothespins to the new swordsman.

LEADER NOTES:
When switching samurais, ask everyone to unclip the clothespins from the previous samurai and add all the clothespins to the new samurai's clothes. Everyone working together will make the transition much faster.

VARIATIONS:
Begin the game with three clothespins on everyone. When the samurai loses all of her clothespins, the person who takes the last pin from the samurai becomes the new samurai and the game continues. If the samurai hits anyone, he or she loses a clothespin that is put aside until the next game.

Foam Foiling

GROUP SIZE:
2 players

TIME:
10 to 20 minutes

PROPS:
• One midaroni or maxaroni sword

OBJECTIVE:
Slice off your opponent's limbs.

HISTORY:
The original version of this game is called "Tote",
which is an ancient German word meaning "death by
duel". The idea was to throw a stick similar to a
broomstick toward your opponent as if it were a
sword. Mike Spiller first introduced me to the game
at one of his Games Of The World workshops.

PREPARATION:
Make a sword by marking one foam noodle nine
inches from an end to identify the "handle" of the
sword. For a more colorful sword, glue a nine inch
section onto a midaroni. Use two colors of course.

SCENARIO:
In a battle to save your planet, you have discovered
that an explosion has caused an earthquake. The
earthquake has separated the hallway between you
and the outside by several feet. The split in the floor
is so deep that you cannot see the bottom.

All of a sudden, an evil Jedi warrior appears at the
other edge of the split. He engages his light saber

and sets it to self destruct. He throws the saber toward you and you catch it by the handle and throw it back at the evil Jedi. The floor is unstable and any footsteps to avoid the light saber might cause the whole floor to collapse into the abyss.

Back and forth you toss it, avoiding the blade that could easily remove an arm or leg.

INSTRUCTIONS:
Stand 10 to 20 feet apart facing your opponent.

You will be taking turns tossing a foam sword underhand toward your partner so that it hits him. Be sure to toss the sword by the handle.

The receiver must not move his feet when the other person throws the sword.

When the sword reaches your opponent, several things may result:
• Sword caught by handle -- no injuries
• Sword is blocked with an arm and caught by the handle -- no injuries
• Sword misses the receiver -- no injuries
• Sword is blocked with an arm and not caught by the handle -- loss of an arm
• Sword hits an arm -- loss of the arm
• Sword hits a leg -- loss of the leg
• Sword hits torso, neck, or head -- death

When the receiver loses an arm, that arm must be put behind his back and not used for blocks, catches, or throws. When a receiver loses a leg, he must balance on one foot.

Ways you win the game:
• Your opponent loses both arms or both legs
• Your opponent is "cut" on the torso, head, or neck
• Your opponent falls or moves his feet or foot during a throw

LEADER NOTES:
This game tends to end quickly until people have had some practice. Let people play with it for a while.

The main skills needed are balance, coordination, and decision making. Some people may have small hands and find that the foam sword is too big to toss underhand. It is okay to let someone throw overhand or with both hands if necessary, however, underhand tosses are preferable.

Spaghetti Stand Off

GROUP SIZE:
2 players

TIME:
20-30 minutes

PROPS:
• 1 Midaroni

OBJECTIVE:
Use your balance and agility to spear your opponent and avoid being speared.

HISTORY:
One of the wonderful properties of the foam noodles is that they sail through the air so well. Like an arrow, they seem to glide toward you, then hit their target without hurting anyone.

We took advantage of the way the noodles can be thrown to create this game of balance and concentration.

INSTRUCTIONS:
You will be throwing a noodle at another player like you would throw a dart, then the other player will be throwing it back at you. The receiving player will try to avoid being hit by the leading end of the noodle. The difficulty is that the receiver can only move one of his feet. The thrower must not move either foot. After the noodle has landed, the new thrower can walk to get the noodle and then move back into his position.

Stand 20 feet from the throwing player. Plant your feet however you prefer and prepare to move out of the way of the oncoming noodle.

Take turns throwing the noodle at each other. Remember, the thrower may not move either of his feet. If a receiver is hit by the end of the noodle or moves both feet to get out of the way, the thrower gets 100 points and takes one step toward the receiver. The receiver then becomes the thrower.

The first person to 1000 points wins the game. Win two out of three games to become champion!

LEADER NOTES:

When the game begins, the two players have plenty of space between them and their reaction times are not so critical. As they score points, the tension increases because the thrower is closer and the receiver has to move more quickly to avoid being hit.

VARIATIONS:

Use two noodles, one for each player, and throw them at the same time.

Play with three people in a triangular set-up. Give each player a noodle. Each player throws a noodle at the same time. If two people throw at the same person, then the receiver can throw both noodles on the next turn and potentially score 200 points on the same turn.

Mars Attacks
(Meatball Mayhem)

GROUP SIZE:
2 to 30+ players

TIME:
5 to 15 minutes

PROPS:
• All the meatballs and minironis available

PREPARATION:
Establish a line or lines that will divide teams from each other (see instructions to determine how you will play the game). Dump out all the Flying Saucers (meatballs) and Asteroids (minironis) on the line or intersection of multiple lines. You're ready to go.

OBJECTIVE:
Be the team with the fewest number of alien crafts or asteroids in your area.

HISTORY:
At the writing of this book, Mars Attacks, Asteroids, and Men In Black were movies playing world wide. We thought the name would suit one of our favorite games as kids growing up at camp. We don't even remember what it was called way back when, but we have heard several names since then. Now it has two more. Pick the one more suitable for your occasion. Like if we were into having some fun at the National Vegetarians Conference surely we would play Meatball Mayhem!

SCENARIO:
You are Men (or Women) in Black, assigned to manage alien immigration on your planet. By decree, all alien ships and space debris must be deported or removed from your planet. Commendations will be given to all officers who end up on the planet with the least number of ships and debris after the deadline. Good luck.

INSTRUCTIONS:
Set a deportation time. We find that 2 to 3 minutes is more than enough for one round.

During deportation time, all officers must stay on

their own planet (within their boundary lines).

Alien ships and asteroids can be sent to another planet by hand or by feet.

When time is called, all airborne objects are allowed to land. Any objects sent after time has been called, must come back to the planet from which it originated.

Harpoon

GROUP SIZE:
2 to 4 players

TIME:
20 to 30 minutes

PROPS:
• 10 Midaronis
• 3 Minironis
• Rope, or tape for two borders

OBJECTIVE:
Throw noodles at minironis to knock them over your opponent's line before he hits the minironis over yours.

HISTORY:
To create this book we bought a few dozen noodles and stored them in the office. Our intern, Renny Cavener, had a hard time keeping his hands off of the new toys. He created this activity that we could (and did) play over and over again.

PREPARATION:
Place two borders parallel to each other and approximately fifteen feet apart. Clear the area between the borders.

Place three minironis near the center of the bordered area as shown in the following diagram.

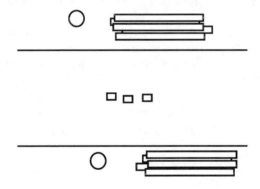

SCENARIO:
It had come down to the two of you. The stink fish had almost overtaken the valley. Now, there were three stink fish in the river between you and your neighbor on the opposite bank.

It wouldn't be so bad if these fish smelled like roses, but these things stunk! Not only did they smell bad, they could crawl on land if they got to the bank.

You and your neighbor each have five stink fish sticks to push the fish to the opposite bank. Only five throws and three fish. Who's going to get the majority of the stink fish stink?

INSTRUCTIONS:
Place three minironis a fair distance between the borders of the play area. You can stack them or lay them in any pattern you like.

Gather five midaronis for each of you and stand outside the borders with your noodles. Once the game begins, you cannot touch the floor past your border, and you must throw the noodle (not use it as a push pole).

When you are both ready, one of you says, "Go", and each of you can throw up to five midaronis at the minironis in the play area.

The player who knocks each minironi over the opposite border gets a point. For example, if Bill and Sheila play the game and Sheila knocks a minironi over Bill's border and Bill knocks one minironi over Sheila's border, each person gets one point. If the third minironi is still between the borders after all the throws are taken, it is not counted.

Play until the first person reaches twenty points.

LEADER NOTES:
Strategy is a major part of this game. At first people try to throw their noodles quickly, then it becomes obvious that someone holding extra noodles after you are done has an advantage. They can take their time to toss the last noodles.

The game works well indoors.

VARIATIONS:
You can use any midaroni that crosses your border. This will give each player the opportunity for more than five throws for each round.

Play with more than one person on each side. Add more midaronis for the additional players.

Form a box boundary with minironis in the center of the box. Now you have four teams. The team with the fewest minironis on its side wins.

Atom Splitters

GROUP SIZE:
10 to 30+ players

TIME:
10 to 20 minutes

PROPS:
- Midaronis (or maxaronis if you have them available)
- Rope to form a circular safe zone

OBJECTIVE:
Unsheathe the noodle between a pair and run to safety before being tagged.

PREPARATION:
Designate a boundary large enough to accommodate your group on a flat playing field. Place a circle of rope approximately 10 feet across near the center of the play area.

SCENARIO:
Today we are going to split some atoms and see what bursts of energy result. Atoms and free radicals make up the players in this nuclear reaction. Who will survive?

Pair up and take a bonding rod that will join the two of you to form an atom as you stand back to back. Try walking around without dropping the rod.

(Let people practice for a short time.)

Two pairs will begin the game as "free radicals" without bonding rods. We will leave the two extra rods in the safe zone. The four free radicals roam the area trying to take a rod from any of the atoms.

Any time a free radical is out of the safe zone, a bonded pair can tag him. If the atoms touch a free radical on the torso (the back, chest, stomach, or waist), the free radical is sapped of his energy and must go to the safe zone to be reenergized.

If a free radical steals a bonding rod from an atom, it releases their bond and they can run to tag the free radical who stole their rod. If they tag him on the torso, he is "sapped" and they get their bonding rod back. If the free radical makes it to the safe zone without being tagged, the partners who were atoms become free radicals.

The only way for a free radical to become reenergized is for another sapped radical to bond with him in the safe zone. The reenergized pair exits the safe zone as a bonded atom. Of course, a bonding rod cannot be taken from an atom in the safe zone.

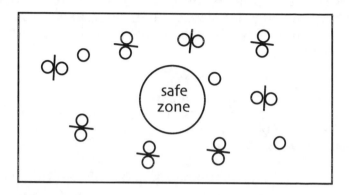

INSTRUCTIONS:
Pair up with someone else in the group. Everyone needs a partner.

Two pairs will need to be the noodle takers, everyone else will be the noodle holders for the moment. Takers move by themselves; holders move as a pair.

Each pair of holders needs one noodle that they will hold with their partner between their backs. No fair holding on to the noodle with your hands.

When we start, each taker will try to take the noodle from between pairs of holders. Then he will run with the noodle to the safe zone before being tagged by the noodle-less pair. At the same time, the noodle-less pair can chase the taker separated from each other.

If the taker makes it to the safe zone before being tagged, the noodle-less pair become takers. The person in the safe zone is free to go out and take other noodles.

If a taker is tagged on the torso before reaching the safe zone, he must give up his noodle to the holders who restore their noodle to its original position. The tagged noodle thief can only get back into action by going to the safe zone and joining with another tagged taker with a noodle. The two tagged takers become a new holder pair.

The game ends when everyone is a holder, everyone is a taker, or everyone is exhausted.

LEADER NOTES:
Maxaronis make this activity easier. The midaronis work well, but the pairs of holders can easily reach out to touch the taker. This is why the tags must be made to the taker's torso.

Once a taker makes it safely into the safe zone, he or she should leave the noodle in the safe zone.

Low Rollers

GROUP SIZE:
4 to 6 players

TIME:
10 to 20 minutes

PROPS:
- 5 or 7 meatballs for each player
- 1 Spot marker for each player

PREPARATION:
Create a circle with spot markers about fifteen feet in diameter. Place spots equal distance apart from each other. You're ready to go.

OBJECTIVE:
A center player tries to avoid rolling discs, while rolling players try to become center player.

INSTRUCTIONS:
The best playing surface for this game will be a flat, hard type surface such as a gym floor or concrete slab. We tried this in the grass once and it was a flop!

Ask all the players to stand on a spot holding 5 to 7 meatballs. Pick a player to be the jumper, then ask her to stand in the middle of the circle. The objective will be to roll the meatballs across the circle trying to hit the player in the center. If a rolling disk hits a jumper, the roller shouts, "hit". The game stops and the jumper trades with the roller. All of the rollers for the next round gather the disks and restart when everyone is ready.

Rolls travel across the ground. Rolls can only be made by a player standing on a spot. Rolling players may enter the center of the circle to get a meatball, but must return to a spot to roll the disk.

Jumpers are only "out" if they are hit by a <u>rolling</u> meatball.

LEADER NOTES:
Add or subtract meatballs if it is too hard to hit a jumper or too easy.

VARIATIONS:

There is a fun option we have tried. The center players are allowed to kick rolling meatballs. However, rolling hits from their blind side change out jumpers.

Gold Digger

GROUP SIZE:
10 to 16 players

TIME:
10 to 15 minutes a game

PROPS:
- 2 Midaronis
- Approximately 7 minironis for each player(yellow for Gold -- if you have different colors call the game Jewel Digger)
- 1 Spot marker for each player
- 4 Hula-Hoops

PREPARATION:
Choose an open playing area large enough to accommodate your group. You will want an area at least 30-feet in diameter. Place the four hoops at the center of the area in a four-leaf clover formation. Choose a top and bottom hoop, and a side by side hoop. In the top and bottom hoops, put an equal number of minironis. In each of the side by side hoops, place one midaroni. Set out one spot marker for each player. The spot markers are placed in a large circle, each approximately 15 feet from the hoops. (See illustration below.) You're set to play.

OBJECTIVE:
Each Gold Digger tries to reach his goal of gold.

HISTORY:
This is another great game from Karl Rohnke. We added the Gold Nuggets to his game to establish a concrete goal opportunity. If you want to try Karl's version, eliminate the Nuggets. Have players "Count Coup" by running into the center, touch their foreheads to the ground, yell, "COUP" (pronounced coo), and return to a spot before getting NOODLED. Any way you play, it's classic fun.

INSTRUCTIONS:
Start out with all players standing on a spot -- these are Gold Diggers. Ask for two volunteers to be "it" -- called Noodlers. Noodlers are not "it" very long. Ask the Noodlers to stand out in the center with a midaroni.

The Noodler's objective is to tag any of the Gold Diggers with a midaroni. By tagging a Gold Digger, the Noodler becomes a Gold Digger and the Gold Digger becomes a Noodler (with us so far? Great!?) Noodlers can tag Gold Diggers at any time during the game. Tags must be below the waste to be considered a transforming tag. A Noodler, after tagging a Gold Digger, must place the midaroni back in an empty hoop after the tag, and then get to an open spot before they become a full fledged Gold Digger.

The Gold Digger's objective is to collect gold (minironis). Each time a Gold Digger leaves her spot, she is allowed to pick up one piece of gold and then return to a spot before getting another piece of gold. Gold must be held in the hands and arms at all times. Players are not allowed to stash their gold anywhere or stuff it into clothing -- oh yah, players are not allowed to give nuggets to another player to hold for them (it happens!). When a Gold Digger is tagged, she must first place her gold (if they have any) back into a top or bottom hoop, then pick up the midaroni left behind by the Noodler, and then proceed to tag a Gold Digger. The Noodler who just tagged the Gold Digger is also fair game. Follow the same rules as the Noodler.

Some specifics: The midaroni must be set in an empty noodle hoop (the side ones) for the transfer to be made. If a Noodler does not get the midaroni into the hoop, the Noodler must come back to correct the error. However, the Gold Digger is still tagged. He calls the Noodler back to correct the error all the while hovering over the midaroni ready to pick it up when it is placed in the hoop (for the inevitable quick-tag-back action -- all part of the fun).

The game stops when the last piece of Gold has been picked up.

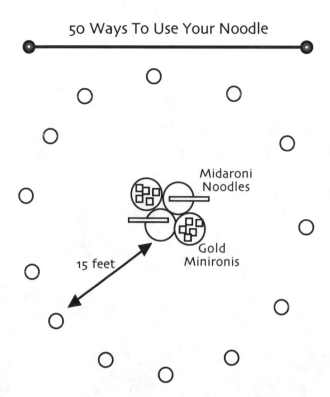

Midaroni
Noodles

Gold
Minironis

15 feet

LEADER NOTES:
If you want to process more than just a fun time,
before the game starts, ask all the players how many
pieces of gold they want to obtain by the end of the
game. When the game stops, find out if the players
reached their goals. Why? Why not?

This game can get quite competitive if you let it. We
find that healthy competition is great as long as
others are not being physically or mentally hurt in
the process. If hurt occurs, the game is no longer
fun.

VARIATIONS:
If you do not have enough minironis, any other small
objects will work. We have even used wadded up
paper and called the game pearl diving.

Trust Run

GROUP SIZE:
12 to 20 players

TIME:
15 to 25 minutes

PROPS:
- 1 Midaroni for every player (a midaronis for each player's hand if you have enough)
- 1 Spot marker for every player

PREPARATION:
Set out two lines of spot markers, across from each other, four feet apart. The space between spot markers in the same line should be about two feet apart.

OBJECTIVE:
Players run through an uplifting line of noodles without slowing down or being touched by noodles.

HISTORY:
This activity comes from the creative spirit of Craig Dobkin. Craig was kind enough to let Chris use the original version in his E.A.G.E.R. Curriculum. We added the noodles for some color.

INSTRUCTIONS:
Give each player a midaroni and ask all of them to stand on the spots in one of the two lines. Have the two lines of players face each other. Players hold the midaroni about stomach high and horizontal to the ground so there is one flat level of noodles when the instructor looks down in-between the lines (the noodles should look like a zipper from a birds-eye view).

From here, the instructor will back up about 15 to 20 feet away from one end of the line (we like to demonstrate this first so the players see that it works -- we hope). Inform the group that you will be running through the middle of the line. Ask the players to lift each noodle up as you get close to it, then lower the noodle as soon as you have passed, like one of those wave motions. Sound effects add to the experience. Star Trek door opening/closing sounds work well.

The runner gives a primal shout, "READY." The lines shout back, "READY." The runner is off in a blaze down the gauntlet of noodles.

With a successful pass, ask who would like to try a run through the noodles. The instructor picks someone and takes her noodle and place in line. "Ready," "Ready," RUN! Continue the process until everyone has had the opportunity to try.

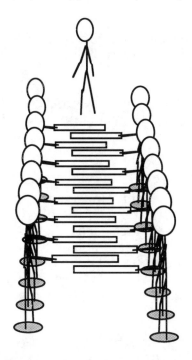

LEADER NOTES:
This activity may be very challenging for some players. It does involve a lot of trust. The first time through they might slow up before getting to the line. We like to give every player at least two tries, one to get used to it, and one to get it.

You might not want to try this activity until the group has a chance to build trust in each other. Finding out what decreases and increases trust are good topics to start to use with this activity.

If someone does get "bopped" with a noodle, find out what caused it. You will have to decide if the activity should continue or if the group should move onto another activity (one that can build trust again).

Pasta Roll

GROUP SIZE:
1 player a roll

TIME:
10 seconds a roll

PROPS:
- At least 20 midaronis (the more the better)
- An open floor
- A pair of those cloth gloves might be good if you have some. The gloves may allow a safer slide.

PREPARATION:
Set out all your midaronis on the floor parallel to each other in a long column, about 4 inches apart from each other. Keep enough floor space out past the noodles to allow the pasta rolling body to travel some distance without hitting any obstruction -- like a wall!

OBJECTIVE:
A player rolls out across the column of noodles as far as possible without touching the floor.

HISTORY:
Our first experiment of Pasta Rolling landed Renny Cavener into a pile of boxes under a table. Consequently, we had to put in the, "keep enough floor space" rule. Even with this rule in place, more of us had to try it -- rolling into the boxes that is. Noodle testing is not for the faint of heart!

INSTRUCTIONS:
Long pants and long-sleeved shirts are highly recommended for this one.

The pre-roll check should include removing glasses and taking off all jewelry and belts that might get caught on the equipment.

The Pasta Rolling enthusiast starts about 10 feet behind the noodle column. Moving towards the column (a fast sprint is not required here; the roller's objective is to stay on the noodles all the way, so a slow run into the noodles will be more than enough for a great ride) the roller will be taking a head-first slide action onto the top of the noodles, arms extended.

Avoid the high flying belly dives onto the noodles. The roller should stay low as she comes in for the landing.

LEADER NOTES:

As the instructor you want to keep things safe. Pasta Rolling has the potential to over-ride the noodles and go skipping across the floor. So the idea is not to over-ride the roll. Using the cloth gloves suggested above will allow the rider to place her hands down on the floor (if the noodles run out) and push the upper body up off the floor preventing skid marks.

? Problem-Solving **?** Activities

Problems or puzzles surround us each day. Where do I want to have lunch? Who can I ask to go with me to the mall? How much am I willing to spend for entertainment? What do I want to be when I grow up? All of these questions take skills to answer well. Even adults struggle with problems.

Problem-solving activities like the ones in this book have a variety of purposes. Like games, problem solving activities can be fun and energizing; however, fun is not necessarily a key part of the solution process. After completing a tough problem, the feeling may be more like satisfaction, confidence, and self-esteem rather than fun. Problem-solving in a "no one is the expert" setting can teach us about who we are and how we handle ourselves around others.

Activities with a problem to solve tend to make people use more of their brain power than their physical strength. This characteristic enables a wide variety of people to participate and succeed.

As a leader, look more deeply into the lessons learned from solving problems with others, because challenges in life do not go away. Enjoy the problem solving activities and remain open to learning something about yourself and others as you join in.

3-D Noodle Shapes

GROUP SIZE:
5 to 15 players

TIME:
15 to 45 minutes

PROPS:
• Midaronis or maxaronis
• Bandannas (optional)

OBJECTIVE:
Arrange all the noodles to outline a specific polygon.

HISTORY:
The blind polygon is a well-known activity that uses rope. We thought the stiffness of the noodles would provide good materials to form two-dimensional shapes as well as three-dimensional shapes.

PREPARATION:
Lay out the number of pieces you need for the shape. (See the diagram for a visual.)

Triangle = 3, 6, 9, 12 . . . noodles
Square = 4, 8, 16 . . . noodles
Pentagon = 5, 10, 20 . . . noodles
Cube = 12, 24 . . . noodles
Three-sided pyramid = 6, 12, 24 . . . noodles
Four-sided pyramid = 8, 16 . . . noodles

SCENARIO:
A curse! You never said anything about a curse!

It was true. The tomb that you found had an inscription that detailed how you would suffer the wrath of the pharaoh, unless you could create the ancient key to survival. The key had to be built with all the cane logs stored in the tomb

All of a sudden the lights in the tomb went out, the opening shut, and you all had to build the key (a three-sided pyramid) in the dark using all the dried cane logs.

INSTRUCTIONS:
Ask everyone to put on a blindfold and listen to the rest of the instructions.

Using all of the noodles available, you need to construct a shape that I will mention in a moment.

You must connect the noodles at the ends and not side by side against each other. Remember that you must use all the materials.

When the group thinks the shape is completely formed, you may take off your bandannas (or open your eyes).

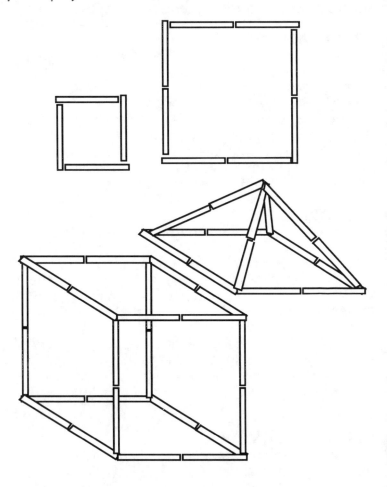

LEADER NOTES:
The bandannas are optional because some people do

not like the cloth over their eyes whereas other people have a hard time keeping their eyes shut and may want a blindfold. The important thing in this activity is that no one can see. They will have to cooperate without their eyesight.

The more noodles you add to the problem, the more complex the solution will be. Consider that the height of the shape must be possible for the group to build without blindfolded people needing to get onto people's shoulders (a safety hazard).

You can have more noodles than people.

VARIATIONS:
Try it sighted, then try a new shape unsighted. Make a large letter of the alphabet instead of a polygon.

Blind Bat

GROUP SIZE:
4 to 30+ players

Times:
3 to 5 minutes a round

PROPS:
- 1 Midaroni for every two players
- 1 Spot marker for every two players
- 1 Blindfold for each player

OBJECTIVE:
Pairs of players communicate with each other to score as many points as possible during the allotted time.

INSTRUCTIONS:
Try to use a creative way to pair up players if they are not comfortable pairing up by themselves. Have each pair obtain 1 spot marker, 1 midaroni, and 2 blindfolds.

Ask the group of pairs to create a large circle. The center area of the circle will be the playing field, so make sure it will be big enough to accommodate the number of bodies that will be playing.

When you have set the boundaries, have the pairs put their spot marker on the ground. This will be their "home base." Complete the remainder of the instructions while pairs are standing at their home base.

During the action of this game, players from each pair will be taking turns being unsighted (blind). They have the choice of using the blindfolds available or simply closing their eyes. (It is important to provide this choice to players. There are people who do not feel comfortable with something over their eyes.)

When the game begins, one player from each pair will go into the center of the circle unsighted and armed with a noodle. The player's partner, while standing on his home base, verbally guides the unsighted partner for a score. A score is made by "batting" another player below the waist.

Here are the stipulations:
1. Each time an unsighted player enters the playing field, he only has one swing to take.
2. All swing actions must occur below the plane of the player's waist.
3. After a swing is made, this player must be guided out of the playing field, still blinded, back to home base. Then, she trades roles with her partner. The sighted becomes un-, and the un- becomes sighted.
4. If a player's swing hits another player below the waist, a point is scored for that pair (the swing player still goes back to home base).
5. If a player is hit, he must be guided back to home base to switch roles -- even if a swing was not made by that player.
6. All players must remain upright on their feet during the game. (Ducking low tends to produce many head bats.)

Set your game time by the development of your group. We have found that the younger the group, the shorter the game time. This surely is not set in stone.

LEADER NOTES:

As you can imagine, this game involves aspects of communication. We like to play shorter rounds with younger groups so we can take the time between games to talk about effective communication strategies. If you find that your group (of any age) is struggling, stop the game to discuss ways of improvement. In other words, if you see it becoming unsafe, please stop the action and find ways to improve safety. Thank you.

DNA

GROUP SIZE:
8 to 20 players

TIME:
5 to 10 minutes

PROPS:
• 1 Midaroni for every player

OBJECTIVE:
The group works together to create the largest circle possible pressing a midaroni between each player and then attempts to invert the circle.

HISTORY:
This activity was contributed by Dr. Jim Cain. He says that the shape made by the group as they invert the circle looks like a DNA molecule -- thus the name.

INSTRUCTIONS:

Have the players hold midaronis between their open palms around a complete circle. Now by moving slowly, have the circle stretch outward until the largest size is reached without dropping any noodles. Remember, only the palms should be touching the noodle. This will encourage communication between participants as they reach their limits. Then shrink the circle to the smallest size, and finally return the circle to the original size.

When the group is ready to increase the challenge, turn the circle inside out without dropping any noodles. We will let groups try this option any way they can -- usually meaning they can touch the noodles with their fingers. When the circle is inverted, ask them to return to the original circle, but this time do not allow fingers to grab the noodle.

LEADER NOTES:

We tried this once with a group of adults and it turned out to be very difficult for some players to "open up" their arms all the way. Don't underestimate the simplicity of this activity. It can be very powerful.

VARIATION:
While inverting the circle, each player must go over or under a different pair of connected hands.

Noodle Up

GROUP SIZE:
10 to 16. (There must be enough players to keep this a safe activity. See LEADER NOTES below.)

TIME:
20 to 30 minutes

PROPS:
• 10 or more midaronis

OBJECTIVE:
Players construct a vertical "pipe" structure as high as their constraints allow.

INSTRUCTIONS:
Provide the group with as many midaronis as available. Ask them to create a vertical tower with the midaronis. The noodles may only touch together on the flat ends. The tower should not be more than 10 degrees off vertical.

Choose the tallest person in the group to be the benchmark. This person must have her feet on the ground at all times. The knees of any other player in the group cannot go above the benchmark's head.

LEADER NOTES:
In almost all cases, groups will put members on shoulders during this activity. It is very important to keep everyone safe if this occurs. Make sure there are two players spotting the person in the air at all times. A spotter should have hands and arms up and ready to protect the shouldered person in case they fall. Members often find this boring because they are not able to get into the action of the tower building. However, it is up to you as an instructor to stress the need for spotting as it relates to the complete success

of the group (e.g., "If someone gets hurt, will we be successful?").

Appoint yourself or someone in the group to be the safety regulation officer (an SRO). This person is in charge of making sure all group members are acting safely.

VARIATION:
Do not mention to the group that the tower needs to be vertical. Try to create the longest diagonal noodle line.

Noodle Up II

GROUP SIZE:
5 to 10 players for each structure

TIME:
20 minutes

PROPS:
- 2 Rolls of masking tape for each group
- 20 or more midaronis for each group
- Camera (optional)

OBJECTIVE:
Build the tallest free-standing, self-supporting foam structure possible in 15 minutes.

HISTORY:
Noodle Up II is an adaptation of Balloon Castles found in the book, *Feeding The Zircon Gorilla*. Instead of balloons and transparent tape, this activity requires noodles and masking tape. The noodles provide the materials to build a much taller, brighter, and impressive structure.

PREPARATION:
Set out two rolls of masking tape along with the foam noodles for each group. Select a variety of colors.

Be sure to select a space where the ceiling is high enough to accommodate a tall structure. If construction will be outside, avoid locations that are windy or have moisture on the ground.

SCENARIO:
The year is 2006 and being a good neighbor has still not gone out of style. New folks have joined the farming community and need a tower raised for their

home-based telecommunications business.

All the specially designed materials have already arrived. It will be up to you and your fellow neighbors to raise the tower. The higher the tower, the better the reception will be. The new folk's parents will be calling them in only 20 minutes, so plan your strategy and get to buildin'.

INSTRUCTIONS:
Take 5 minutes to plan as a group how to build the tallest free-standing, self-supporting foam structure you can, using the foam and the two rolls of masking tape.

No one may touch the materials until the 5 minutes of planning have passed. You will have 15 minutes of construction time.

LEADER NOTES:
Watch the team or group build the structure. Did it look like what they had planned? What roles did people take? Was the base strong enough to support the mountain of foam? How did they overcome the height barrier when the structure was too high at the top to reach? If there was more than one team, how did competition show itself?

Spot anyone who leaves the ground if the group chooses to lift someone to add extra height to build their structure.

Regardless of how it looks in the end, each group likes a picture next to their creation.

VARIATIONS:
Build different types of buildings (e.g., fort, house, pyramid, space ship).
Give the group more time or materials.
Ask the group to construct the structure so that the <u>way</u> it is built has meaning.

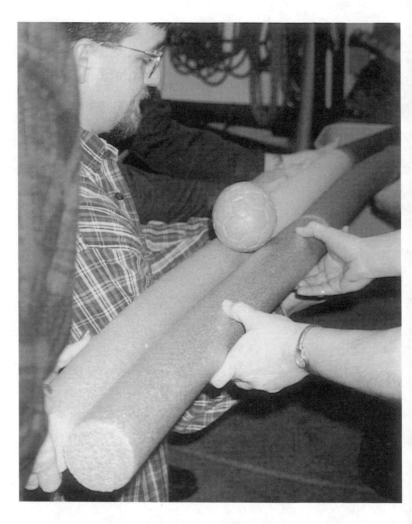

Immobile Chopsticks

GROUP SIZE:
10 to 20 players

TIME:
15 to 45 minutes

PROPS:
- Enough midaronis for all but 2 players
- 2 Kitchen tongs (or use another prop for the "vertical movers" -- You could even specify certain noodles as vertical movers)
- 1 Container (e.g., basket or tub)
- A lot of round objects that have roll potential (what about an egg or two?)
- 1 Rope to mark out a circle boundary

PREPARATION:
Place the container in the center of the playing area. The area does <u>not</u> need to be an open space or free of obstructions. Place the rope on the ground so that it forms a circle boundary around the container, no more than a 4 foot radius. You can be the judge if the boundary needs adjustment. Place all the rollable objects in various spots around the playing area. If trees or other above-ground locations are available, place the rollables in the branches and nooks as well as the ground.

OBJECTIVE:
Players work together to move the rollable objects from their resting place into the container.

HISTORY:
This activity was contributed by Clay Fiske, the Challenge Course Coordinator (C cubed for short), for Summer Summits, Inc in Denton, Texas. He discovered this game, in its miniature form, at a local Chinese restaurant where his boss makes him eat all the time. While picking up his garbanzo beans with his chopsticks, the bean would roll down along the chopsticks before he could get it in his mouth. To eat the bean, he would have to lift his hand up to roll the bean down into his mouth. The light bulb lit and the fireworks went off. The time came for a great game.

SCENARIO:

With youth groups, especially peer leaders, we say that the rolling objects represent other youth who need help in some way or another. The container represents the counselor's office. It will be the player's task to help these youths reach the counselor. If you choose (as we often do) to use a bowling ball, this may represent a child who, no matter how hard you try, won't budge or accept help from others. (We have seen some groups develop ways to move the bowling ball, so don't count on anything until the game is over.)

With corporate groups, we state that the rollables are clients that are becoming disillusioned with the group's company. How can the group get them "back into the bank?"

INSTRUCTIONS:

All participants must utilize one resource -- a midaroni or tongs. Once each participant has a resource, he may not touch another resource.

Midaronis represent horizontal movers. The tongs represent vertical movers. The idea is to get as many rollables as possible into the container by using the available resources. The rollables may not be rolled along the ground at any time. No body part may come in contact with the rollables. Tongs are used to pick up the rollables from the ground or out of a nook -- but remember, tongs can only move objects up and down. The noodles are used to move rollable forward, backwards, or side to side, but not up and down.

Example: A player uses the tong to pick up a ball from the ground. A team of noodlers stations itself under the rollable so the object can be placed on the noodles to be moved towards the container.

"Now for the wrenches," says Clay. When a rollable is

in contact with a noodle or tong, the player(s) holding said noodle or tong may not move his feet. If a rollable is ever dropped while in transit, either vertically or horizontally, it must be returned to its starting point -- on or above the ground. (The instructor can place the rollable back in its spot, or the group could be made to place it back with their resources.) As for the rope boundary, no body part or resource may touch any surface inside the circle -- yes, this means the container may not be moved.

LEADER NOTES:
I usually ask the participants to set a goal as to how many rollables they can get in the container within a certain amount of time. Facilitators can also help with quality control (or following the rules) by sounding an alarm, "beepbeepbeepbeep" whenever a rule is broken, (e.g., tongs moving a rollable sideways, or the participant's feet moving when their resource is in contact with the rollable).

VARIATIONS:
Chopsticks -- This was Clay's first game. The tongs are eliminated -- all the rest of the props are used the same way. Players are asked to pick up a midaroni with one hand. Then they are given one minute to decide which hand they want to use and where they want to hold onto the noodle. When the time is up, players may not move their hand from that spot on the noodle and may not use their free hand to assist transportation in any way. No body part may touch the rollables. Players may transport a ball any way possible, except for rolling it along the ground. They may also move their feet during transport.

Dot To Dot

GROUP SIZE:
2 to 15 players

TIME:
10-20 minutes

PROPS:
• Several meatballs or minironis

OBJECTIVE:
Hold as many sections of foam between yourself and a partner as you can.

HISTORY:
For all those people who like to play Twister or People To People, here is the game for you. This activity came out of our game creation session for this book. We decided it could have two versions: partners or groups.

PREPARATION:
Lay piles of meatballs or minironis where each pair or group will be connecting their dots.

SCENARIO:
It is the future and you want to play the latest virtual reality game. The kid down the block just downloaded this program and says it's great. Unfortunately, you know what kinds of difficulties there still are to download a massive program of this sort.

You are going to have to make a solid computer chip connection with this kid in order for the program to download into your cells. The more chip connections you can hold, the more realistic the program will seem.

INSTRUCTIONS:
Get with a partner. You will try to hold as many meatballs and/or minironis as you can between the two of you.

The limits are as follows:
Only your feet may touch the ground.
Both you and your partner must be touching each noodle slice (no stacking).
Clothing may not assist holding the pieces (you cannot stuff your shirt, pants, or tie any pieces together).

LEADER NOTES:
Provide a safe place to play this game. Move away from any hard objects with corners or points. Sometimes people fall down because they lose their balance.

VARIATIONS:
Try it with a group. Give each person five meatballs to start before adding more. Everyone must connect to at least two other people and the group has to connect overall -- no loose ends.

Full Circuit

GROUP SIZE:
8 to 25 players
The number of meatballs may limit group size. (See PREPARATION.)

TIME:
20 to 30 minutes
The size of the group will effect the time.

PROPS:
• A bunch of meatballs
• Lots of minironis.

PREPARATION:
We like to count out 4 meatballs for every adult player and 3 meatballs for every youth player in the group (hand size is a factor). This is not written in stone. The group does not need to know that you set out 3 or 4 meatballs for each of them. Place all the meatballs in a large pile. You will also need a bag full of minironis, more than enough to place one in-between each meatball.

OBJECTIVE:
The group must use all the meatballs (called "chips" in this game) available, each separated by a minironi (called "caplets" in this game) to form a complete circuit above the ground.

SCENARIO:
You are a group of electrical specialists called upon to restore power to the blacked-out metropolis of (use the city name from whence the group hails). The main power plant was overloaded during the President's State to the Union Address. The insulating Fiber-Con capsules disintegrated, leaving only the power grid chips to be used again. Fortunately you have with you the latest breakthrough in insulating chips -- Ultra Fiber-Con caplets. Your mission is to reconstruct a full circuit that will restore the city's power. Your construction manual has the following stipulations...

INSTRUCTIONS:
All the Chips must be used in the circuit to restore full power.

Chips cannot be touching each other when the circuit is completed, so a Fiber-Con caplet must be placed in-between each chip. The caplets and chips cannot have any flat to flat connections.

The Fiber-Con caplets are highly fibrous. Human

contact with the caplets can be highly debilitating. The fibers can even go through clothes. Be very careful!

The circuit must be off the ground (or floor) for maximum power. When the circuit is complete, a steady flow of power should be able to continue through the circuit indefinitely.

LEADER NOTES:
You may place yourself in the position of "Quality Controller" or appoint a person in the group to be QC. This person will determine whether the circuit can provide maximum power based on the instructions.

Debilitating effects of the caplets will be up to the challenge level of the group. (e.g., blindfolding a player who touches a caplet, losing the use of one hand, etc.)

VARIATIONS:
Include in the instructions that the circuit must also be at two different levels to add additional power for the growing needs of the town. See what happens.

Three Towers

GROUP SIZE:
2 to 6 players

TIME:
15 to 30 minutes

PROPS:
- 50+ Meatballs and/or minironis
- 1 Hula-Hoop or other boundary marker for each group

OBJECTIVE:
Build towers out of foam. The objective of the facilitator (if there is a facilitator) is to observe the interaction of the participants.

HISTORY:
This game was developed as an observation tool for small group interaction and decision making. We often find that even the simplest games bring out valuable information.

PREPARATION:
Lay a circular boundary, such as a rope or hula-hoop, on the ground for the towers. Place numerous meatballs and minironis on the floor near the boundary.

SCENARIO:
Welcome to The Circle, a global observatory for highly intelligent people. Today we will be observing your construction skills so that builders can learn newer and better ways to design the homes of the future.

We are focusing our efforts on homes with three supports, so please let no more than three building blocks touch the floor. Also, take turns placing each block so that we will have the combination of your efforts.

When any of the building blocks fall to the floor, stop and let the observers take note of the building before you start over.

INSTRUCTIONS:
Get into a group of two to six and sit around the circle.

Build a structure with no more than three pieces touching the floor.

Players take turns making <u>one</u> of three possible moves on each round:
1) Add a new piece to the structure from outside of the circle.
2) Move one piece already within the circle.
3) Move one stack of pieces already within the circle.

The structure(s) must stand on its own.

The game starts over when any piece of the structure falls to the floor.

LEADER NOTES:
The striking observations facilitators often notice in this activity are the patterns of behavior in each of the players. Some players continue to add to the structure while others move the pieces to "fit" with their own version of how this thing should look.

Each person is free to choose any of the three types of moves available, yet there may be a sense that once a piece is set, it must stay there. In truth, anyone can move any one of the pieces or stack of pieces when it is his turn.

Some players may change the design of the structure by moving the pieces, while others may try to verbally influence the other players' moves.

Some of the following questions may be appropriate: What was your goal? Who was the leader? What would it have looked like if you had done it by yourself? How did the other players change the way it looked when the tower was finished?

VARIATIONS:
Build the widest structure you can.
Build the tallest structure you can.
Build the strongest structure you can. Test it with a full soft drink can.

Make a "snarfle" trap. Snarfles are particularly
attracted to foam.
Play non-verbally.

Funky Dunk

GROUP SIZE:
4 to 8 players in a working team

TIME:
5 to 10 minutes a dunk

PROPS:
- 1 or 2 Midaronis for each player depending on ability
- Basketballs or volleyballs, at least 1 for each working group

PREPARATION:
Indoor Basketball Court: Place all the basketballs you want to use on the half court line.

Outside Court: If there is no center line, place the basketballs in one central location between the hoops you will be using.

OBJECTIVE:
Working teams transport a basketball from its stationary spot, using only the midaronis, then place the ball into the hoop for a point.

HISTORY:
We had a great name so we had to make up a great activity to go with it.

INSTRUCTIONS:
The only thing that can touch the basketball is the midaroni. Each midaroni can only be held by one end with one hand, and this hand must be at least 1/2 a midaroni length away from the ball at all times. (You can't just have that hand right up there next to the ball -- challenge yourself!)

All working team members must have midaroni contact with the ball during transit. All transit action must take place above the ground (no rolling the ball). If the ball drops in transit, the group must start over from the spot where the ball first bounced.

If the ball touches any other object, like body parts, during transit, the group must start from the basketball's original position.

LEADER NOTES:
The degree to which you hold fast to the rules will depend on how much you want to challenge the players. Sometimes we will blindfold them if they touch the basketball. This always adds an interesting twist.

If you coach basketball, this is a great cross-training teamwork activity. We like to focus on how players work together on a different sort of problem. (Then, we surely have to throw in some of those running and chasing noodle games just for fun.)

Noodle Walk 1

GROUP SIZE:
8 to 15 players

TIME:
15 to 30 minutes (depending on the distance of the walk)

PROPS:
• 1 Midaroni for each player

OBJECTIVE:
The group must travel from point A to point B without breaking the noodle connections with one another.

SCENARIO:
You are a group of specialists gathered together to dispose of some toxic waste containers discovered by some vacationers back in the woodlands of a small island off the coast of Florida. Only two containers are leaking from one end; the rest are leaking from both ends. To contain the leaks, the ends of each container must be pressed against each other during transportation. If at any time during transportation the front end of any specialist's container becomes disconnected from another container, that specialist must reconnect with a different container (reconnecting with the same container may cause oximorphicrebiofication resulting in accelerated toxic leakage). Containers may never be reconnected to each other once they have been disconnected (e.g., If container 3 disconnects from container 2, these two cannot be reconnected in that order). Also, to prevent any subcutaneous skin damage, specialists may not hold directly over the connecting points of the containers. Your leakage expert will be available for any consultations on disconnection during

transportation.

INSTRUCTIONS:
The prior scenario covers most of the ground rules. The group should be allowed to figure out the additional limitations (such as: the noodles with one end leaking will be at the front and back ends of the line).

Another stipulation added for high functioning groups would be to disallow any contact of other noodles but the specialist's own (you can't physically touch any noodle except the one you start with).

LEADER NOTES:
You can choose to be the leakage expert (LE), or ask one of the group members to be. If one of the goals of this group is quality, the LE's job will take on a very important role. If the group has a hard time with authority, taking this role yourself could give the group a chance to work on appropriate behaviors in this area.

This activity is a bit more challenging than you might imagine. Start out with shorter walks to establish an understanding of how this works for you.

VARIATIONS:
This activity could be combined with Noodle O's. The group could make a large horizontal O and then try to move the O from one place to another without the ends detaching.

Noodle Walk 2

GROUP SIZE:
6 to 15 players

TIME:
15 to 30 minutes depending on the length of the walk

PROPS:
• 1 Midaroni for each player except for the leader

OBJECTIVE:
The team of players travels without losing any noodles, from point A to point B, each separated by the length of a midaroni.

INSTRUCTIONS:
Gather the group together. Before explaining the activity to the group, ask them to choose a "task manager". Assure the group that the activity will not

involve any physical risk and the task manager has the opportunity to be changed at any point in time during the activity.

When the task manager is chosen, ask the other players to get a noodle (the task manager will not have one to start with).

Explain to the group that they will need to get from the starting to the ending point (that you have established), traveling with a single noodle in-between each player. When the group is in motion, the noodle ends may only touch a player's abdomen and back areas. No player will be allowed to hold the noodle or to use any other resource to hold the noodle in place (e.g., you can't tuck the end of the noodle in your garments) and all the noodles must be used.

If a player's noodle (the one in front of them) becomes dislocated from the line, the line must stop and this player must move to the back of the line and reconnect before the line continues to move.

LEADER NOTES:
As in Noodle Walk 1, this activity is a bit more challenging than it appears. You might want to avoid this one with newly formed groups. Communication is the major issue here. If they have trouble communicating, this activity may be very difficult.

Another fun consequence we have used is turning the player around after dropping a noodle (walking backwards in the line) -- very tough.

Spaghetti & Meatballs

GROUP SIZE:
8 to 20 players

TIME:
15 to 30 minutes

PROPS:
- 1 Midaroni for each player
- Meatballs (number will depend upon group size --
  See INSTRUCTIONS.)
- A long activity rope for boundary line
- 1 Spot marker for each player.

PREPARATION:
Create a large circle boundary with the rope -- this
will be the bowl of sauce. Around the bowl, set out a
spot marker for each player -- these spots will be the
plates. Set the plates equidistant from each other.
The meatballs will go out into the sauce after the
group decides on the number of falls into the sauce.
(See INSTRUCTIONS.)

OBJECTIVE:
Each player must cross to the opposite side of the
bowl of sauce, without falling in, ending up standing
on a new plate with a noodle and a meatball.

INSTRUCTIONS:
Each player starts out with one noodle and stands on
one of the plates. In this position, explain to the
group that when they are ready, they must start
where they are now. From here, they will need to
cross the sauce and end up on another plate across
from them with a noodle and a meatball.

The only objects that float on the sauce are the
noodles and meatballs. Each time someone falls into
the sauce a meatball splashes out (take one from the
bowl).

With all of this in mind, ask the group to tell you how
many falls in the sauce they will need to have a
successful crossing. For example, if the group tells
you they will have no more than 5 falls into the sauce,
put out a meatball into the sauce for each player and
5 extras. Now the bowl of sauce is filled with

meatballs all scattered about.

Once the meatballs are placed in the sauce, the game can begin. If the group exceeds (for example) their 5 fall ins, the activity is over and the group will have to reassess the process and try to solve the limitations they had to be more successful in the next crossing.

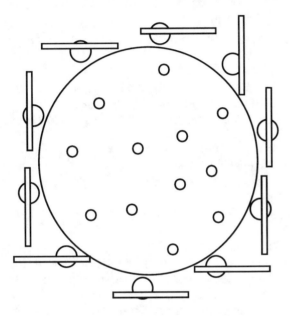

LEADER NOTES:
You and/or the group will have to decide what a "fall into the sauce" means. Will it be a complete foot stepping into the sauce or just a toe touch?

Through our experience with this activity, we have found it best on the integrity of the noodles to do this one in stocking or bare feet. Shoes tend to damage the foam. This often limits our playing field to indoors. However, if you have a safe outdoor area, go for it.

Noodle O's

GROUP SIZE:
10 to 18 people

TIME:
20 to 30 minutes

PROPS:
• As many midaronis as available

OBJECTIVE:
Within the safety limits and size of the group(s), make the largest vertical "O" shape possible with only the flat ends of the midaronis touching each other. (Safety is very important during this activity. See LEADER NOTES.)

INSTRUCTIONS:
Hand each player a midaroni and then ask him to pair up and create an "O" shape. With success, ask if they want a grander challenge. Yes, of course!

Ask each pair to pair up with another pair. Create an "O" shape with the four midaronis in the group. If they make their "O" horizontal, ask them to move it vertical. Success!? But of course . . . Ask them if they would like another . . .

If the group is large enough, ask the fours to get into eight's. Can a vertical "O" be created safely within the group? (Safety will require a "Benchmark" and "Spotting." See LEADER NOTES below.)

OR

Ask the entire group to get together and fashion the largest vertical "O" within the safety guidelines. See if the group can keep the shape within 10 degrees of vertical (or best estimate...but of course).

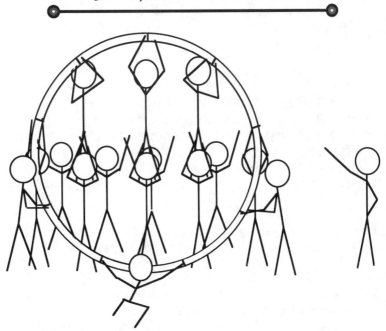

LEADER NOTES:

When groups move into the, "getting on the shoulders stage," choose the tallest person in the group to be the "Benchmark." This person must have her feet on the ground at all times. The knees of any other player in the group cannot go above the benchmark's head.

In all cases so far, groups will put members on shoulders during this activity to gain the height advantage. So it is very important to keep everyone safe if this occurs. Make sure there is someone "Spotting" the person in the air at all times. A spotter should have hands and arms up and ready to protect the shouldered person in case of a fall. Members often find this boring because they are not able to get into the action of the tower building. However, it is up to you as a leader to stress the need for spotting as it relates to the complete success of the group (e.g., "If someone gets hurt, will we be successful?").

Appoint a safety regulation officer (SRO). This person is in charge of making sure the group members are safe.

Some points you may want to watch for:
What is the "Quality" of the "O", when the group has completed?
Is the finished product acceptable to all the group members?
Is everyone in the group a part of the finished product?

VARIATIONS:
If you decide ahead of time, or if you are working with a smaller group, try to construct the tallest Noodle Arch.

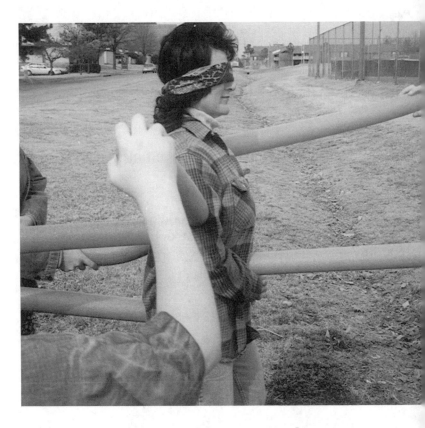

Noodle Nudge

GROUP SIZE:
4 to 6 players for each group

TIME:
10 to 15 minutes

PROPS:
- 1 Midaroni for each person
- Obstacles for the course like meatballs or any other type of noodle
- 1 Blindfold for each team

OBJECTIVE:
Move each member of your team through an obstacle course using the foam noodles.

PREPARATION:
Lay out an obstacle course for each relay team.

SCENARIO:
In each of our lives there are many obstacles that slow us down and cause us to go in circles. Fortunately, we have friends, family, peers, and others who help guide our lives. They cannot live our lives for us, but they can nudge us in the right directions.

Each of you is about to start down a path. Because none of us can see the immediate future, you will be blindfolded and guided by your friends. They will not be able to travel for you, however they can influence your journey and coach you along.

INSTRUCTIONS:
Divide the group into teams of up to six people. Give each team a noodle for all but one person and a bandanna for the person with no noodle.

When the race begins, the sighted members will guide their blindfolded team member through the obstacle course. When the first person completes the course, a second person puts on the blindfold and the team goes again. The race is completed when the last blindfolded person finishes the course.

Only the blindfolded person can touch the ends of the noodles. Be careful not to let the blinded person fall down; it could hurt her and it will slow down your race speed. The noodle holders must hold the noodle at the end farthest away from the blindfolded person.

If any member of the team touches an obstacle, the team must guide the blind person once around the object for each touch before continuing the course.

LEADER NOTES:
People wearing blindfolds tend to move more slowly than sighted people. The temptation of the sighted members of the team is to push the blinded person too quickly. Caution everyone about this and encourage everyone to practice with a person's eyes closed a few minutes before the relay.

Feel free to make the obstacle course any way you want. Objects to step over or duck under add another level of challenge since no one can touch an obstacle without consequences.

VARIATIONS:
Instead of a relay race, have the team guide a person through a building.

Try it silently.

Blindfold the outside people and have the center person sighted to guide them. Contact with the ends of each noodle must be maintained.

Worm Walking

GROUP SIZE:
2 to 30+ players (if you have lots of noodle stuff)

TIME:
10 to 30 minutes

PROPS:
- All the midaronis, minironis, and meatballs you have
- Some type of boundary markers -- a few ropes or some cones
- 1 Blindfold for each player

PREPARATION:
Create a large rectangle boundary area. The size will depend on how many players you will have and how many noodles and meatballs (we call them worms and slugs) are available. Spread out all your worms and slugs within the boundary area (see INSTRUCTIONS to understand the task -- this may help you determine where you place the props).

OBJECTIVE:
Players guide their unsighted partners through the muck without touching any of the worms or slugs.

HISTORY:
Since we have all of these great props we couldn't resist adding this time honored Karl Rohnke classic. This activity is great for developing communication skills between two people. There is always a lot to talk about after this one.

SCENARIO:
You are a group of technical advisors traveling through the jungles of South America on foot. In your way is a toxic fuming bog filled with direction

altering worms and slugs. To cross the bog, you must wear some protection over your eyes (blindfolds). Since your eyes will be covered, you will be guided by another player from the safety of the near bank. When you reach the other side, you will need to take off your eye protection and guide across the person who guided you. Stay on the far bank in safety. If at any time a player would touch a direction altering worm or slug, the crosser's directions are altered by 90 degrees (e.g., if a player is walking forward and touches a prop, this player turns 90 degrees -- having to walk sideways. If the same player touches another prop, this player, turning another 90 degrees, will now be walking backwards and so on). Good luck to all of you. I'll see you on the other side.

INSTRUCTIONS:
Ask players to partner up. If there is an odd number, you can play or create a group of three.

The idea here to verbally direct partners through the maze of obstacles. Sighted partners are not allowed in the bog area.

To keep the group somewhat together, make sure all the first crossers reach the far bank before they start to bring their partners over.

LEADER NOTES:
There will be a number of things to talk about after this activity, such as; What made it difficult? Did anyone devise a strategy or any special communication during the crossing? How did you feel when you or your partner touched an obstacle? What did you find helpful during the crossing? Why is communication important?

If we have the time, we like to cross the smaller width of the bog first. This allows a bit more room to move and takes less time to cross. Then we move to cross the longer length way. With the practice of the first crossing and some brainstorming after, this challenge is a good one for practicing what was learned.

VARIATIONS:
If you have access to <u>unused</u> mousetraps, set them and add them to the bog -- call them snapping turtles (don't play this variation barefoot!).

Stick Games

GROUP SIZE:
2 to 12 players (or more if the interest is focused)

TIME:
10 to 20 minutes

PROPS:
- A few midaronis -- the number will depend on which stick games you use

OBJECTIVE:
Players work on lateral thinking skills to solve stick puzzles.

HISTORY:
Stick games have been around for many years. Since we have the great jumbo sticks, we thought it beneficial to spark the idea for you. If you want to add more of these mind-busters to your bag of tricks, dig around at your local library.

LEADER NOTES:
We use these activities mostly as educational time fillers. When we have a few minutes during breaks when people start wandering back, we throw some noodles on the ground and get the minds working again. These stick games can also be great programming pieces. Lateral thinking is a valuable tool in our complex society.

All you need to do with the stick games is set up the noodles according to the diagrams below, then just read the players the directions.

Triangles. Set up 9 noodles as shown. Move 3 of the noodles to make 5 triangles.

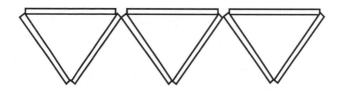

Squares. Set up 8 noodles as shown. Take away 2 noodles and leave 3 squares.

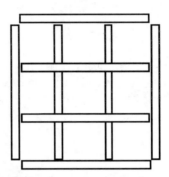

Sum. Set up 10 noodles as shown. Move just 1 noodle to make the sum work out correctly.

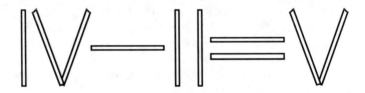

(Solutions are found on page 193)

Who

GROUP SIZE:
8 to 16 players

TIME:
10 to 20 minutes

PROPS:
- 1 Midaroni for each player
- 1 Blindfold for each player

OBJECTIVE:
Players try to identify one another by communicating only with two noodles.

HISTORY:
This esoteric activity was developed by Dr. Jim Cain.

INSTRUCTIONS:
While blindfolded, each player will be partnered up with another player by an instructor/helper. Each player will hold onto the opposite end of their partner's midaroni. When the instructor says to begin (no movement until the game begins), without talking, players attempt to determine the identity of the other person they are working with. Participants cannot let go of the noodles, but may use any creative and safe techniques available to identify the other person (such as tugging on the noodle to determine the strength of the other player, lifting the noodle to determine the height of the other person, etc.).

Each round will last one minute. When the instructor says stop, each player states the name of the player they think they have been working with. After the chatting dies down, instructors/helpers move players to new partners and start a new game. Play as long as the interest remains.

LEADER NOTES:
We use this activity with groups after they have had a substantial amount of time getting to know each other and getting to know some of the qualities that make each person unique.

It works well to have a few helpers in this activity to

move players to new partners after each round.

After the games are over, talk about some of the strategies the players used to identify each other. You will be amazed how creative some people get.

Just About Right

GROUP SIZE:
6 to 12 players

TIME:
10 to 15 minutes

PROPS:
- Several midaronis, minironis, and meatballs -- more pieces than the number of players
- 2 Cones or 2 gallon water jugs full of water

OBJECTIVE:
Using only a single prop per participant, choose the optimal number and lengths of noodles to just fill the space between the two targets.

PREPARATION:
Before the group arrives, set out the two cones or jugs as targets (or any other two objects that can be fitted with noodles). We like to form fit the number of props needed to just fit between the targets to obtain the correct spacing between targets (e.g., if your group has 12 members in it, place 12 props of different lengths in-between the targets so it appears to be solved, then remove all the props and leave the targets to be filled again by the group).

INSTRUCTIONS:
When the group arrives, do not allow them to get close to the targets. Set out the props you have fitted earlier along with several extra props some distance away from the targets. In this way participants will be required to use their estimating skills to solve the problem.

The group will have to stay near the props while only a single player is allowed to place his noodle piece.

This player must return to the group before the next player can run to place theirs. As stated in the OBJECTIVE, each player can make only one placement to reach a solution.

Several different targets can be used for multiple tries so that the ability of the group to estimate distances can be improved with practice.

VARIATIONS:
Allow each player to have an option of moves:
1. Place a noodle between the targets.
2. Move a noodle within the target.
3. Remove a noodle from the target.

Go for the least number of moves to solve the puzzle.

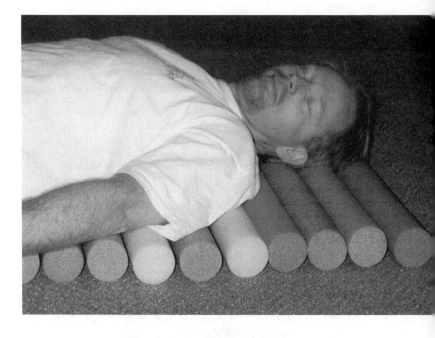

Pasta Massagta
(massage-ta)

GROUP SIZE:
1 Massagter at a time

TIME:
As long as needed

PROPS:
• About 10 midaronis -- body size will influence
  numbers

PREPARATION:
Set out the noodles parallel to each other, about 1
inch apart, in a long column.

OBJECTIVE:
Reach a state of relaxation and contentment.

INSTRUCTIONS:
After a long day of noodling, it's time to relax. Set the noodles out as instructed. Lie down with your back on the noodles. Your feet will be flat on the floor with your knees in the air (shoes are required for a solid anchor point). Using your feet as an anchor point, slowly push your body forward and pull it back along the top of the noodles to get that magic full body massage feeling. After a few minutes of this, you'll be ready for more action.

ANSWERS TO STICK GAMES:

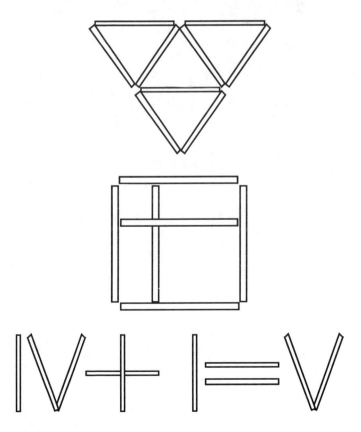

Chris Cavert

Chris has been working and playing in the Human Services field since 1979. He received his undergraduate degree in Physical Education and is currently preparing to conclude his graduate work in Experiential Education. Chris is a nationally known speaker in the areas of "Adventure Based Activity Development" and "Games and Play" to enhance pro-social and educational programming.

His other published works include the, *E.A.G.E.R. Curriculum: Experiential Activities, Games, and Educational Recreation* * *Games (and other stuff) for Group* books 1 & 2 * *Games (and other stuff) for Teachers* * and *Affordable Portables: A Working-Book of Initiative Activities & Problem Solving Elements.* For information about these publications contact Wood-n-Barns Publishing at 1-800-678-0621.

For workshop and additional information, contact Chris at Chris@FunDoing.com

Sam Sikes

Sam is the Founder of DoingWorks, Inc. in Texas, a training organization that specializes in experiential learning techniques.

Sam trains, facilitates, and speaks nationwide in a variety of corporate and educational settings including Fortune 500 companies, small businesses and universities. Best known for his creativity, Sam has trained groups of as few as two people and as many as three thousand. He certifies Ropes Course facilitators and develops related indoor and outdoor training activities for adults. He is active in organizations such as the Association for Experiential Education and the American Society for Training and Development. In 1996, Sam was recognized as "Practitioner of the Year" in a five-state region for his achievements in training by the Association for Experiential Education.

Sam holds a Master's Degree in Industrial/Organizational Psychology from the University of Tulsa, and a Bachelor's Degree in Psychology from Texas Tech University in Lubbock.

His published materials include:
Feeding the Zircon Gorilla ✳ *Executive Marbles* ✳
Virtual World ✳ *Equestrian Knights of Uma* ✳ *50 MORE Ways to Use Your Noodle* ✳ and *Raptor.*

For workshop and additional information, contact Sam at, 512•778•6640, Sam@DoingWorks.com or Sam@LearningUnlimited.com

Additional Contributors

We want to thank these special people for their contributions to this book and their contributions to the world at large.

Karl Rohnke is one of the most widely known Adventure Activity writers in the field of Experiential Education. His generous sharing touches players of all ages and from all over the globe. For more information about Karl's publications, contact Kendall/Hunt at 1-800-228-0810.

Mike Spiller began Games Of The World in Hawaii in 1984. Today he has collected over 5000 interactive games from his travels to over 21 countries. Mike hosts a Treasure Chest of Ideas Conference and a Clown Circus Camp annually. He has concentrated most recently on traditional Native American games and European Pub games. For workshop information, contact Mike at Rt 3 Box 82A, Giddings, TX 78942 (409) 542-5902.

Dr. Jim Cain is the author of the award winning adventure-based text *Teamwork & Teamplay*, which recently received the Karl Rohnke Creativity Award presented by the Association for Experiential Education. He is the Executive Director of the Association for Challenge Course Technology, and manager of the Cornell University Corporate Teambuilding Program For more information contact Jim at, 468 Salmon Creek Road, Brockport, NY 14420, (716) 637-0328, fax- (716) 637-5277 E-mail- jimcain@teamworkandteamplay.com

Craig Dobkin has served on the Board of Directors of the Association for Experiential Education and currently is the President of the Youth Biz Board, an

entrepreneurial business program for inner city youth. Craig is a co-founder of Play for Peace, an organization that brings children of conflicting cultures together through play. Craig currently works with the West Pines Training Center. For more information on how you can help support Play for Peace, contact Craig at 228 W. Sycamore Ln., Louisville, CO 80027.
E-mail, craigdobkin@playforpeace.org

How to Contribute to Future Books

Do you have new
Games?
Problem-Solving Activities?
Pictures?

Send information to:
"Noodle Book"
Learning Unlimited Corporation
5155 East 51st Street, Suite 108
Tulsa, OK 74135

-or-

Contact us by:
phone   (918) 622-3292
fax   (918) 622-4203
e-mail   Sam@LearningUnlimited.com

Ordering more books and supplies . . .

To order additional books contact us at:

Learning Unlimited Corporation
5155 East 51st Street, Suite 108
Tulsa, OK 74135
(918) 622-3292
(918) 622-4203 fax
Sam@LearningUnlimited.com

Need Noodles?

We can refer you to all the noodles
you need. Just contact us and we
can put you in contact with cutters
of noodles whole and already cut
and bagged.

MasterCard, Visa, & American Express
accepted

Cover Design
Jim Weems at
Ad Graphics

Photography
Chris Cavert
Sam Sikes

Text and Layout
Skia font
ClarisWorks 3.0
Macintosh Powerbook 520c

Editing Assistance
Sharon Kremer

EXPLORE THESE PLACES FOR MORE INFORMATION:

Association For Experiential Education
2305 Canyon Blvd, Suite 100
Boulder, CO 80302-5651
303-440-8844
www.princeton.edu/~rcurtis/aee.html

National Society For Experiential Education
3509 Haworth Drive, Suite 207
Raleigh, NC 27609-7229
919-787-3263
nsee@datasolv.com
www.tripod.com

American Camping Association
5000 State Road 67 North
Martinsville, IN 46151
1-800-428-2267

Kendall/Hunt Adventure Education Catalog
4050 Westmark Drive
Duduque, IA 52004-1840
1-800-228-0810

Game Kids
2280 Grass Valley Highway, Suite 181
Auburn, CA 95603-2356 USA
www.gamekids.com